PINKFLOYDTHEMUSICANDTHEMYSTERY

Copyright © 2010 Omnibus Press
(A Division of Music Sales Limited)

Cover and book designed by Fresh Lemon
Picture research by Jacqui Black

ISBN: 978.1.84938.370.7
Order No: OP53372

Exclusive Distributors
Music Sales Limited, 14/15 Berners Street, London,
W1T 3LJ.

Music Sales Corporation,
257 Park Avenue South, New York, NY 10010, USA.

Macmillan Distribution Services,
56 Parkwest Drive, Derrimut, Vic 3030, Australia.

Picture credits:
p26, p65, p79, p89 & p113 Jill Furmanovsky/LFI; p22 –
p23, p28, p38, p45, p53, p57, p61, p70, p73, p83,
p90, p119 & p153 LFI; p96 & p140 Pieter Mazel/LFI;
p134 Sam Emerson/LFI; p4 Marc Sharratt/Rex Features;
p126-127 Dezo Hoffman/Rex Features; p139 Brian
Rasic/Rex Features; p24, 76, 123 & 150 Getty Images;
p33, 104 & 143 Andrew Whittuck/Redferns; p34 & 137
Chris Walter/WireImage; p37 Gems/Redferns; p41, p42,
p84, p110, p130 & p154 Jan Persson/Redferns; p50
David Redfern/Redferns; p54 & p67 Jorgen
Angel/Redferns; p58 DR H J Dibbert/Redferns;
p62, p69 & p133 Richard E. Aaron/Getty Images;
p74, p103 & p159 Jeffery Mayer/WireImage; p80 Peter
Still/Redferns; p87, p99, p100 & p109 Rob
Verhorst/Redferns; p107, p116, p146 & p157 Harry
Goodwin

Colour section:
p1 Richie Aaron/Redferns, LFI, Jan Persson/Redferns;
p2 Michael Ochs Archive/Getty Images, Adam Ritchie/
Redferns; p3 Chris Walter/Wire Image, Andrew
Whittuck/Redferns, Ray Stevenson/Rex Features;
p4 Michael Ochs Archive/Getty Images; p5 LFI, Peter
Still/Redferns; p6 Andre Csillag/Rex Features, LFI; p7 MJ
Kim/Getty Images, News (UK) Ltd/Rex Features; p8 Geoff
Robinson/Rex features, Ivan Chernichkin/Reuters/Corbis,
Brian Rasic/Rex Features, Peter Andrews/Corbis

Printed by Guttenberg Press Ltd, Malta

A catalogue record for this book is available from the
British Library.

Visit Omnibus Press on the web at
www.omnibuspress.com

PINK FLOYD
THE MUSIC AND THE MYSTERY

ANDY MABBETT

OMNIBUS PRESS

LONDON / NEW YORK / PARIS / SYDNEY / COPENHAGEN / BERLIN / MADRID / TOKYO

INTRODUCTION PAGE 23

PART I
THE GROUP RECORDINGS PAGE 29

TIMELINE >>>

PART II
SOLO RECORDINGS PAGE 127

1943
SEPTEMBER 9

Roger Waters born in Great Bookham, Surrey.

1965
JANUARY

Billed as The Tea Set, a group comprising Barrett, Waters, Mason, Wright and Bob Klose make their debut appearance at Uxbridge.

1944
JANUARY 27

Nick Mason born in Birmingham.

1946
JANUARY 6

Roger (Syd) Barrett born in Cambridge.

1945
JULY 28

Rick Wright born in London.

1964

Various groups containing future members of Pink Floyd appear in London under the names Sigma 6, The Abdabs, The Screaming Abdabs and Spectrum 5.

1946
MARCH 6

David Gilmour born in Cambridge.

1965

Klose leaves in the summer and for the remainder of the year the group alternate between calling themselves The Tea Set and The Pink Floyd Sound.

1967
LATE JANUARY

Pink Floyd record their first single, 'Arnold Layne', at EMI's Abbey Road Studios, which will be released in March.

1966
OCTOBER 15

Pink Floyd are effectively introduced to the London Underground at the *International Times* First All Night Rave at the Roundhouse.

1967
FEBRUARY

Pink Floyd begin work on their debut album, *The Piper At the Gates Of Dawn*. Recording sessions continue during the next three months.

1967
APRIL 29

Floyd play the 14-Hour Technicolour Dream at London's Alexandra Palace, alongside 30 other groups.

1966
LATE OCTOBER

Peter Jenner and Andrew King of Blackhill Enterprises become Floyd's managers. Together with booking agent Bryan Morrison they attempt to find a record label for them.

1967
MAY 12

Games For May is the chosen title of Pink Floyd's triumphant concert at London's Queen Elizabeth Hall.

1967
JUNE

Pink Floyd's second single, 'See Emily Play', reaches number six on the charts.

1968
MARCH 1

Syd's departure is officially announced by Blackhill who opt to manage him and turn the management of Pink Floyd over to Steve O'Rourke who previously worked as an accountant at their booking agency. O'Rourke will manage the group until his death in 2003.

1967
AUGUST 4

Floyd's debut album, *The Piper At The Gates Of Dawn*, released.

1967
NOVEMBER 4

Pink Floyd open their first US tour in San Francisco.

1967
NOVEMBER 14

Pink Floyd join a UK package tour with Jimi Hendrix, The Move and others.

1968
JANUARY 20

Syd Barrett makes his last appearance with the Floyd at a show in Hastings. Thereafter the group settle into life as a quartet with Waters, Wright, Mason and newcomer Gilmour.

1967
DECEMBER

David Gilmour joins the group on guitar, briefly making it a five-piece.

1969
APRIL 14

Pink Floyd follow up dates around the country with a headlining appearance at the Royal Festival Hall, London.

1968
JUNE 29

Pink Floyd headline the first ever free concert in London's Hyde Park. Also on the bill are Tyrannosaurus Rex, Roy Harper and Jethro Tull.

1968
JULY

Second US tour.

1969
JULY

Soundtrack to *More* released.

1969
MAY

National UK tour opens in Leeds.

1968
JUNE 28

A Saucerful Of Secrets album released.

1969
AUGUST 8

National Jazz & Blues Festival, Plumpton Racecourse, Sussex.

1970
MARCH

Antonioni's film *Zabriskie Point*, with soundtrack by Pink Floyd, is premiered in New York. The album is released in May.

1969
NOVEMBER 7

Ummagumma released.

1970
JUNE 27

Pink Floyd perform in front of an audience of 150,000 at the Bath Festival, a three-day event headlined by Led Zeppelin.

1970
JANUARY 2

Syd Barrett's first solo album, *The Madcap Laughs*, is released.

1970
APRIL – MAY

US tour.

1970
OCTOBER 2

Atom Heart Mother released.

1970
JULY 18

Another free concert in Hyde Park.

1971
OCTOBER/NOVEMBER

The group embark on their most extensive North American tour to date.

1971
NOVEMBER 5

Meddle released.

1971
MAY 15

Pink Floyd play the Garden Party at London's Crystal Palace Bowl, a set which climaxes with an inflatable monster emerging from the lake in front of the stage.

1972
JANUARY 20

Dark Side Of The Moon is premiered at a concert in Brighton, England, a full 14 months before the album will be released.

1970
NOVEMBER 13

Barrett, Syd's second solo album, is released.

1971
OCTOBER 4-7

Pink Floyd are filmed performing in a Roman Amphitheatre in Pompeii, Italy, for the movie *Pink Floyd Live At Pompeii*.

1971
AUGUST 6

The Floyd open their first Japanese tour in Hakone, followed by their first dates in Australia.

1973
JANUARY/FEBRUARY

Floyd play a series of shows in France with the Roland Pettit Ballet Company, performing live for eight concerts while a further eight used a recorded playback of their music.

1972
OCTOBER 21

Floyd play Wembley Empire Pool in London.

1974
JUNE

French tour.

1972
JUNE 2

Obscured By Clouds released.

1973
MARCH 23

Dark Side Of The Moon released while the group are in the midst of a lengthy North American tour. It will become one of the world's best-selling albums.

1974
NOVEMBER - DECEMBER

UK tour.

1973
MAY

Two concerts at Earls Court Arena in London.

1975
JUNE

Sessions commence at Abbey Road for *Wish You Were Here*. Syd Barrett, by now living quietly back in Cambridge, makes an unexpected appearance.

1977
MARCH

UK tour opens with five consecutive concerts at Wembley Empire Pool.

1975
APRIL

US tour.

1975
SEPTEMBER 12

Wish You Were Here released.

1976

For the first time since their formation Pink Floyd go a whole year without performing live.

1975
JULY 5

The Floyd headline the annual Knebworth Park all-day event.

1977
JANUARY 21

Animals released on the eve of a European tour.

1979
DECEMBER 1

'Another Brick In The Wall, Part 2' becomes Pink Floyd's first and only number one hit single in the UK. It remains at the top of the charts through Christmas and into the new decade.

1978

Again, Pink Floyd do not perform live for a whole year but the final quarter is spent recording *The Wall*.

1979
NOVEMBER 30

The Wall released. Rick Wright is not credited as a member of the band.

1977
APRIL-JULY

North American tour includes four nights at Madison Square Garden, New York.

1978
SEPTEMBER

Rick Wright releases his first solo album, *Wet Dream*

1980
FEBRUARY 7-13

The Wall is performed over seven consecutive nights in Los Angeles, with the band augmented by Rick Wright and four additional musicians.

1978
MAY

David Gilmour releases his first solo album.

1979

No concerts, just recording sessions.

1981
JUNE 13-17

A repeat performance of *The Wall* concerts are staged at Earls Court. This would be the last time the four-man Pink Floyd played together until 2005.

1980
JULY 4-9

The Wall is performed over six nights at Earls Court in London.

1982
JULY 14

Premiere of the film *Pink Floyd - The Wall.*

1980
FEBRUARY 24-28

The Wall is performed over five nights at Long Island Coliseum.

1983
MARCH 21

The Final Cut released.

1984
MARCH

David Gilmour's solo album *About Face* released.

1981
FEBRUARY 13-20

The Wall is performed in Dortmund, Germany.

1981
MARCH

Press reports indicate that Pink Floyd are suing financiers Norton Warburg for negligence. Apparently Norton Warburg has lost £2.5 million of the band's money on unsafe investments.

1984
APRIL

David Gilmour tours
Europe with his own band.

1984
JUNE

David Gilmour tours the
US with his own band.

1984
JULY

Roger Waters begins touring
worldwide with his own band,
which includes Eric Clapton on
guitar. His set includes solo and
Pink Floyd material.

1984
MAY

Roger Waters' solo album
*The Pros And Cons Of
Hitch-Hiking* released.

1986
OCTOBER

Roger Waters drops his application
to prevent David Gilmour and Nick
Mason from using the name Pink
Floyd. Henceforth Pink Floyd and
Waters will tour separately, though
both will continue to perform songs
from Floyd's back catalogue
together with new material.

1985
JULY 13

David Gilmour appears at
Live Aid at Wembley
stadium, playing guitar
with Bryan Ferry's band.

1985
AUGUST

Nick Mason's solo album
Profiles released.

1985
OCTOBER

Rogers Waters applies to the High
Court to prevent the name Pink Floyd
being used again.

1987
SEPTEMBER 7

A Momentary Lapse Of Reason released.

1988
JULY- AUGUST

European tour includes two nights at London's Wembley Stadium.

1987
NOVEMBER

Roger Waters tours the US and plays two shows in London.

1988
JANUARY-FEBRUARY-MARCH

The new-look Pink Floyd tour New Zealand, Australia and Japan.

1987
SEPTEMBER 9

The first Pink Floyd tour without Waters on bass opens in Ontario, Canada, and continues throughout the US until mid-December.

1988
APRIL-JUNE

North American tour.

1987
JUNE

Roger Waters' solo album *Radio KAOS* released.

1989
MAY-JUNE

European tour.

1994
MARCH 30-JULY 18

The US leg of the *Division Bell* tour opens in Florida. For this tour Gilmour, Wright and Mason are augmented by eight extra musicians.

1990
JUNE 30

Pink Floyd appear at a charity event at Knebworth, England.

1990
JULY 21

Rogers Waters presents an all-star version of *The Wall,* outside at Potzdamer Platz in Berlin, featuring several guest artists in front of an audience of 250,000.

1988
NOVEMBER 21

The live album *Delicate Sound Of Thunder* released.

1992

Roger Waters' solo album *Amused To Death* released.

1994
MARCH 28

The *Division Bell* released.

1994
OCTOBER 12

The opening night of an unprecedented two-week run of concerts at Earls Court is halted prematurely when a section of seating collapses.

2002
FEBRUARY-JUNE

In various stages Rogers Waters tours South America, the Far East and Europe, concluding with a show at the Glastonbury Festival in the UK on June 29.

1996
OCTOBER

Rick Wright releases his album *Broken China*.

1999
JULY 23

Now billing himself as 'The Creative Genius of Pink Floyd' Waters takes to the road in the US for an arena tour.

1996
JANUARY 17

Pink Floyd are inducted into the Rock And Roll Hall of Fame at a ceremony in New York.

1999
SEPTEMBER

David Gilmour plays guitar in Paul McCartney's 'Rock and Roll' band at a handful of gigs in the US and UK.

1994
JULY 22-SEPTEMBER 25

European tour.

2003
NOVEMBER 14

Gilmour, Mason and Wright, with Dick Parry, perform three songs together during the funeral service for Pink Floyd manager Steve O'Rourke at Chichester Cathedral.

2005
JULY 2

David Gilmour, Nick Mason and Rick Wright reunite with Roger Waters for an emotional four-song set for Live 8 in London's Hyde Park. Midway through the performance Waters says: "We're doing this for everyone who's not here, particularly, of course, for Syd."

2006
MARCH

On An Island, David Gilmour's third solo album, is released. Gilmour's solo concerts in the UK, the rest of Europe and the USA feature Rick Wright on keyboards.

2006
JANUARY 6

Syd Barrett dies after a long illness.

2003
NOVEMBER 7

David Gilmour appointed Commander of the Order of the British Empire "for services to music".

2006
JUNE-JULY

During Roger Waters' summer festival tour in Europe Nick Mason plays drums at selected dates. Most shows feature a complete performance of *Dark Side Of The Moon*.

2008
MAY

David Gilmour awarded an 'Ivor' for Lifetime Achievement by the British Association of Composers and Songwriters.

2009
NOVEMBER 11

Anglia Ruskin University of Cambridge and Chelmsford award David Gilmour an Honorary Doctorate for his outstanding contribution to music as a writer, performer and innovator.

2008
SEPTEMBER 15

Rick Wright dies from cancer.

2008
SEPTEMBER 22

David Gilmour releases *Live in Gdansk*.

2008
SEPTEMBER

Fender Guitars make available a David Gilmour Signature Black Strat model.

2006
SEPTEMBER

Roger Waters' tour takes in the USA.

INTRODUCT

A few years ago, I – like a good many other people – would have bet a very large sum of money that Pink Floyd – the post-1987 group, comprising guitarist, singer and undoubted leader David Gilmour, drummer Nick Mason and keyboard player and occasional singer Richard Wright – would never reunite with bassist and singer Roger Waters, no matter what the cause. How wrong I was, and how unexpected the lump in my throat as, watching them on television, in public together in Hyde Park in July 2005 for the first time since I saw them at the film première of The Wall in 1982, I was proved mistaken. It didn't matter that Waters' voice was past its best, or that Gilmour had been so determined not to be bested by his arch-rival and former band-mate that he had practised his solos until his fingers were sore. After the event, he described the reunion as being like sleeping with an ex-wife. From where I was watching, it was more like meeting up with an old girlfriend, and finding that, though she has raised a family with someone else, and gained a few silver hairs, and would never be with you again, her smile could still conjure up fond memories of your shared past and make your skin tingle. On that Saturday night, the tide really did seem to have turned.

ON

Briefly, it seemed, there was a glimmer of hope that the foursome might actually go on to perform further, full-length, concerts together, but any slim chance of this happening was dashed by the sad death of Rick Wright in September 2008. Every Pink Floyd fan will have mourned their quiet, unassuming keyboard player, whose vast contribution to the sound of Pink Floyd was so eloquently recalled by both Gilmour and Waters in the heartfelt statements they released following his death.

If Wright's passing served to set a final seal on the career of Pink Floyd, the death the previous year of Syd Barrett was equally mourned, albeit for different reasons. Barrett's withdrawal from music had long ago become a source of intrigue, one of the most mystifying sagas in rock, but his contribution to the group as their first singer, guitarist and songwriter was crucial to there ever being a Pink Floyd in the first place. Syd might not have played much of a role in the classic recordings Pink Floyd produced in the Seventies, but everyone – not least the group themselves – long ago realised that all this might never have happened were it not for Syd's initial inspiration.

As pioneering users of stage lighting, quadraphonic concert sound, theatrical stage shows and a hundred and one technical and artistic innovations, Pink Floyd have never accepted the words "can't be done" from their collaborators. Such eagerness to embrace the new would be empty bravado were it not matched with thoughtful, meaningful lyrics and stories, exquisite musicianship and, not least, damn fine tunes. That's not to say there haven't been lapses; as we shall see, they have had their share of turkeys, but even these have been produced with style.

I've included enough of the band's history to give context for the music, which is what this book is all about, but if you want to know the full story... well, no one can know the full story apart from the people who lived it, and even they don't agree about some of it. Can you remember exactly what *you* were doing and saying, ten, twenty or more years ago?

Briefly: David Gilmour, Roger "Syd" Barrett and George "Roger" Waters (and, indeed, several other people who will crop up as the story unfolds) all knew each other from their school days in the early Sixties in Cambridge. While Gilmour spent his late teenage years busking and gigging (and getting arrested) in France and Northern Spain, Barrett attended college in Cambridge and Waters studied in London, where he met fellow architecture students Nick Mason, son of a well-known director of motoring films, and Richard "Rick" Wright, a part-trained classical musician with jazz tendencies.

They formed a series of groups, eventually bringing in Barrett (who was also now in London, his artistic talents having earned him a place on a painting course). These short-lived bands went under various names, including The Meggadeaths, Sigma 6, The (Screaming) Abdabs, Leonard's Lodgers (Leonard was indeed their landlord) and The T-Set, before settling on the name The Pink Floyd Sound, which, as every Seventies schoolboy knew, was taken from two of Barrett's favourite bluesmen, Pink Anderson and Floyd Council. As their confidence grew, they went from pop and R&B covers to their own extended psychedelic improvisations, loved by the "freaks" of the emerging underground movement in London but hated by straighter concert goers everywhere else.

What subsequently gave the band such a large and loyal following, and kept the albums selling in phenomenal quantities, was a combination of factors – the innovations, the attention to small detail and quality, the superb music, the cleverness of Waters' concepts and their relevance to everyday life, the mystery that grew around their reluctance to be photographed or interviewed for much of the Seventies, the lack of singles during the same crucial period, the imaginative album packaging, the crisp live sound, the spectacular theatrical shows – and, of course, a special magic that

cannot be copied no matter how much money or equipment is available.

If you want to know *more* of the band's story, there are plenty of places to find it, not least Nick Mason's own *Inside Out* (Weidenfeld & Nicolson, 2004, ISBN 978-0-297-84387-0). Readers are also referred to the recently updated *Crazy Diamond – Syd Barrett and The Dawn Of Pink Floyd* (2007, ISBN 978-1-84609-739-3) by Mike Watkinson & Pete Anderson and *Pink Floyd - A Visual Documentary* (1994, ISBN 978-0-7119-4109-0) by Miles and myself, both of which are published by Omnibus Press.

The other essential Pink Floyd biographies are *Bricks In The Wall* by Karl Dallas (Baton Press, 1987, ISBN 978-0-933503-88-5, but re-published in America in 1994 with a shamefully inaccurate, ghost-written update, without Dallas' knowledge), the late Nick Schaffner's *Saucerful Of Secrets* (Sidgwick & Jackson, 1991, ISBN 978-0-283-06127-1)

and, of course, Vernon Fitch's mind-bogglingly detailed *The Pink Floyd Encyclopedia* is a mine of facts and figures for Pink Floyd train-spotters (and other authors, mea culpa!). Guy Pratt's witty *My Bass And Other Animals* (Orion, 2007, ISBN 978-0-7528-7631-3) is also worth a read, for its descriptions of life on the road with Gilmour and co.

Reference is made throughout the first half of this book to the band's BBC *In-Concert* recordings and sessions. The former originally took the form of shows performed in the BBC's Paris Theatre, London and recorded for later broadcast, although these days they tend to be recorded, or broadcast live, from any suitable venue on a band's itinerary. The sessions are a different beast. Bands have, since before Radio One's creation in 1967, used the BBC's studios to record tracks for broadcast, usually reprising recent albums or singles. In a few cases, though, bands have chosen to air new material, perform cover versions (but not in Pink Floyd's case) or try out numbers which were sometimes quietly forgotten. Readers interested in this influential, but often overlooked, aspect of British popular music culture could do worse than read Ken Garner's superb *In Session Tonight* (BBC Books, 1993, ISBN 978-0-563-36452-8). Although the band and their management consistently and disappointingly refuse to sanction their official release, most of their sessions are available on bootlegs.

In fact, there is far more unreleased material lurking in various vaults than the band would have us believe, and it's time they released more of it, not least because the bootlegs that are available are often of very poor quality, and do both musicians and fans a disservice.

Early in their career, the band members joked that one day technology would have advanced to the point where they would send out employees to oversee performances on their behalf, while they stayed at home. These days, a whole evening's worth of Floyd covers are performed by a host of full-time Pink Floyd "tribute" acts around the globe, including The Australian Pink Floyd Show, who were asked to perform at David Gilmour's 50th birthday party and who have their own ersatz-Floyd live CDs and DVDs, the latter wittily complete with flying kangaroos instead of pigs. Some of them do so in venues which Pink Floyd once made their own, and several of these bands perform whole albums in their entirety. Some even play tracks which Pink Floyd have never performed live, such as 'Not Now John'. There are some purists who ague that that's what the Gilmour-Mason-Wright group, with an ensemble of aides, and Roger Waters, ditto, were doing. That's an extreme view, but it is arguable that – good though much of the post-1982 material has been – neither camp has managed to reach the heights of creativity they achieved together. Whether they could have done so without enduring the creative tensions which eventually tore them asunder after just fifteen years of commercial recording, is something we shall never know. Perhaps the brightest candles do indeed burn shortest.

Pink Floyd's journey from being an improvising, blues-based psychedelic bunch of students, darlings of Sixties London's underground scene, to a stadium-filling monster, not only covers prisms and flying pigs, but also hit singles, tantrums, writs, an underwear thief, minor aristocracy, a roadie's morning ablutions, two operas (one by Bizet, the other a bass player), a World War One veteran, a World War Two veteran, cosmonauts, musical wine glasses, several divorces, a naked porn star, *Chitty Chitty Bang Bang*, too many early deaths, expensive cars, singing dogs, some mental breakdowns, benign Cambridge nepotism, a very nice boat, and Shakespeare. On the way, they lost a madcap, gained a superlatively talented guitarist, and fell out badly. Oh, and made some rather good records. This is *their* story...

Information and assistance for the earlier version of this book was freely and kindly supplied by Vernon Fitch, Aaro Koskinen, Alain Lachaud, George Loaf, Bruno MacDonald, Danni Ryan, Ivor Trueman, Dave Walker and Kev Whitlock and my thanks still go to all of them, as it does to the small army of record, book and video company press officers who assisted with both editions. Adrian Banham has again done a superlative job – all the more amazing considering his inexplicable *disinterest* in Pink Floyd – spotting my typos and errors of grammar. If any remain, please write to him, not me: he doesn't get much post. Of course I also thank my editor, Chris Charlesworth, not only for the money, but for his forbearance, and his fascinating music-business-insider tales of saying "hello" to members of Pink Floyd. Nothing else, just "hello". You have to humour him.

Where I've given timings (e.g. 2'38" means 2 minutes, 38 seconds) these are approximate, and are taken from my CD player's display – yours may vary. Catalogue numbers and release dates are for the UK unless otherwise stated.

A selection of useful web addresses, relating to the contents of this book, is available at **www.pigsonthewing.org.uk**

I hope these essays will enable you to hear the records with the same pleasure they've given me, whether you're an avid fan wanting in-depth knowledge, or a novice seeking guidance.

Andy Mabbett
@pigsonthewing

In memory of Julie Powell and Carole Walker.

PART I
THE GROUP RECORDINGS

The First Demo

THE FIRST DEMO

(Unreleased)

The earliest known Pink Floyd recording session, at a studio in London, took place around Christmas 1964, while jazz guitarist Bob "Rado" Klose was still with the band. The tracks were three Syd Barrett songs: 'Lucy Leave' (which was performed at some of the band's 1966 concerts); 'Double O Bo' (described by Nick Mason as "Bo Diddley meets the 007 theme") and 'Butterfly', plus a cover of the blues standard 'I'm A King Bee'. A limited number were pressed as vinyl acetates, to be given to potential concert venues as evidence of the band's capabilities. 'Lucy Leave' and 'I'm a King Bee' have been bootlegged, and fans eagerly await the appearance of these tracks on a formal release.

A snatch of 'I'm A King Bee' is heard in the background of *The Pink Floyd And Syd Barrett Story* documentary, with much better quality than the bootlegged version.

TONITE LET'S ALL MAKE LOVE IN LONDON

Originally released circa 1968 as Instant INLP 002
CD: See For Miles SEE CD 258

Pink Floyd's first recording session intended for commercial release was on 11 and 12 January 1967, in Sound Techniques Studio, London. Syd Barrett's then girlfriend persuaded film director Peter Whitehead to fund the sessions, produced by the legendary Joe Boyd, where the band cut two of Barrett's songs, 'Arnold Layne' and 'Let's Roll Another One', and two lengthy instrumental jams, 'Interstellar Overdrive' and 'Nick's Boogie', the latter pair being much closer to their contemporary live performances. Only very short extracts of 'Interstellar Overdrive' were used in *Tonite Let's All Make Love In London*, the film for which the tracks had been intended, and on the original soundtrack LP.

Since October 1966, the band members had been part of an equal, six-way partnership,

Blackhill Publishing, with their managers, Peter Jenner and Andrew King. The latter pair took the two short songs from Whitehead's sessions to EMI subsidiary Columbia, who were sufficiently impressed to sign the band and have the songs re-recorded as their first single.

In 1990, See For Miles Records acquired the original master tape of the two instrumentals, covered in green mould. Fortunately, it was wound so tightly that the playing surface of the tape was unaffected and they were able to release an extended soundtrack album, featuring the short clips of 'Interstellar Overdrive' together with the full 16 and 3/4 minute version, plus the previously unreleased 'Nick's Boogie'. The two long pieces were also available on an EP (See For Miles SEA CD4) and a poster-sleeve variant (SFM 2). Both the EP and album include (different) dialogue extracts from the film, and the album also has music by other artists. The original movie, in which Pink Floyd are briefly glimpsed, was also available on video (PFVP 2). On all these releases, 'Interstellar Overdrive', a group composition, is erroneously credited to Barrett alone, and is a different version from the one released later by EMI. 'Nick's Boogie' is credited as a Pink Floyd composition. All formats are mono.

Pink Floyd London 1966/1967 (Snapper SMADVD049), is a region-0 NTSC DVD with a recut film comprising both these tracks, set to additional footage from the recording session, clips of a Floyd gig at the UFO Club (the "headquarters" of the psychedelia scene in London, where Pink Floyd were effectively the house band), mixed Sixties scenes and film, not of Pink Floyd, shot at the *14 Hour Technicolour Dream* event on April 29, 1967, at which they did appear. It has the original mono soundtrack and an enhanced 5.1 version.

THE PIPER AT THE GATES OF DAWN

Released 5 August 1967
as Columbia SCX 6157
UK Chart: #6; US Chart: n/a
First CD: CDP 7 46384 2
Remaster: EMI 8 31261 2;
17 October 1994
Mono CD: EMI 859 857 2;
4 August 1997
40th Anniversary set 27 August 2007
as EMI 503919 2 (3CD)
and EMI 503923 2 (2CD)

There are those who regard Pink Floyd's début as their best album. It is so far removed from *Dark Side...* and *The Wall* that it is hard to believe they were recorded by the same band. Indeed, in many ways, they weren't; the manic, erratic, unpredictable and unreliable Syd Barrett was clearly their leader and, unlikely as it may now seem, Richard Wright was the second most dominant force musically. For a record that is every bit as much a product of the swinging Sixties as any of its contemporaries, it is remarkable that *Piper...* hasn't dated anywhere near as much as its vintage would suggest. No doubt the absence of "Make Love Not War" and drug themes plays a large part in this.

The English whimsy which many attribute to the album is first evident from the title, taken from a chapter in Kenneth Grahame's *Wind In The Willows*, required reading for all Barrett-o-philes.

Barrett, his mental state deteriorating by the day as the pressures of stardom, and no doubt his copious intake of LSD, took their toll, was notoriously difficult to work with, changing tunes and lyrics between – and during – takes.

The album's producer, Norman Smith, was then best known as the engineer on every Beatles album up to and including *Rubber Soul*, and it was only his work with Pink Floyd that kept him from working on *Sergeant Pepper's Lonely Hearts Club Band*, which was being pieced together in an adjacent studio at Abbey Road. At one point during the sessions Paul McCartney stopped by to listen, and in a subsequent press interview described the Floyd's début album as "a knockout". Much of the technical jiggery pokery which created the sound on *Piper...* was learned by Smith through his work with The Beatles although, listening to the playout on 'Bike' or the panning on 'Interstellar Overdrive', it's intriguing to think what he would have made of the album had he had access to a modern, digital studio. One quirk of late Sixties recording practices is the simultaneously released mono version (Columbia SC 6157), which is substantially different from the stereo mix we all know and love.

A second Barrett-composed single, 'See Emily Play', is not on the album, but was added to the Japanese release (Toshiba/ EMI EMS 50104), which also had a lyric sheet. It was also on the original US version, available in mono and stereo (Tower T 5093/ ST 5093 respectively), with a different tracklisting: 'See Emily Play'; 'Pow R Toc H'; 'Take Up Thy Stethoscope & Walk'; 'Lucifer Sam'; 'Matilda Mother'; 'Scarecrow'; 'The Gnome'; 'Chapter 24'; 'Interstellar Overdrive'. Later releases in both countries have reverted to the UK tracklisting.

The front cover was an embarrassingly gimmicky group photo, taken with the aid of a multi-image filter given to photographer Vic Singh by Beatle George Harrison. Barrett

designed the better, Rorschach inkblot-like group silhouette on the rear of the sleeve. Sadly, this is reduced in prominence, and cropped, on the 1994 re-issue, although the new version does offer vastly improved sound quality and many extra photographs.

Piper... was re-released in December 1973, with *A Saucerful Of Secrets*, as one half of the vinyl *A Nice Pair* package (Harvest SHDW 403), cashing in on the success of *Dark Side Of The Moon*.

A 30th anniversary mono CD was issued by EMI in 1997, but did not use the same mono mix as the 1967 mono LP. It came in a textured box, with art cards and with a six-track bonus disc, *Pink Floyd/ 1967 – The First Singles* (described below).

The 40th anniversary of the original release of *Piper...* was marked, a little belatedly, on August 27, 2007, by the release of a special new three-disc edition. This was a book-like package designed by Storm Thorgerson, with a 12-page reproduction of a Syd Barrett notebook. The first two discs contained stereo and mono versions of the full album, each remastered by James Guthrie. The third disc included bonus tracks, including the three 1967 singles, 'Arnold Layne', 'See Emily Play' and 'Apples And Oranges', plus the B-sides 'Candy And A Current Bun' and 'Paintbox'. It also featured the alternative take of 'Interstellar Overdrive', previously only available on an EP in France, and a previously unavailable 1967 stereo version of 'Apples And Oranges'. No mention was made of the legendary "lost" (and widely bootlegged) tracks 'Scream Thy Last Scream' and 'Vegetable Man', which, although recorded for the October 1967 BBC session, remain unreleased, much to the dismay of fans. At the same time, the single-disc version of *Piper...* was withdrawn, and replaced with a two-CD set, having both mono and stereo mixes, without the booklet or the extra tracks.

ASTRONOMY DOMINE

(Barrett)
The first voice heard on the album, reciting the names of astronomical bodies through a megaphone, belongs to Peter Jenner, one of the band's original managers. The opening Morse code, said to be gibberish, soon gives way to sweeping organs, echoey guitars and rat-tat-tat drumming, the like of which few listeners could have previously experienced, even in 1967. And is there early evidence of Barrett's paranoia in the lyric "Stars can frighten"?

'Astronomy Domine' was recorded again in 1969, for the live half of *Ummagumma*. The Canadian version of *A Nice Pair* manages to use this live cut instead of the original. After it was dropped from the live set in June 1971, Pink Floyd fans the world over expressed great surprise when this Barrett composition was resurrected for Pink Floyd's 1994 tour of America and Europe, performed, to a backdrop of oil-slide lights and all, by just the three veteran Floyds with Guy Pratt adding bass. It even gained a second live release, as the B-side of their 'Take It Back' single. Clearly still a band favourite, it was included on the *Echoes* compilation in 2001, and, live, on *P*U*L*S*E* and two David Gilmour DVDs.

LUCIFER SAM

(Barrett)
Partly about Syd Barrett's Siamese cat and partly about his girlfriend Jenny, referred to as "Jennifer Gentle" in the lyrics. The "left side/right side" line refers to the division between the logical and creative functions of the respective hemispheres of the brain. Despite the very "Sixties" tone of the guitar and organ, like that on most of the album, the song still sounds fresh and vital today.

MATILDA MOTHER

(Barrett)
Syd Barrett's role-play as a frightened child, not wanting its mother to put out the light after a bed-time story, uses some of his most eloquent and poetic writing. Interestingly, Syd returned to live with his mother when his pop career ended, remaining very close to her until her death in 1991.

Richard Wright's organ provides a typical example of what Peter Jenner christened "one of his Turkish Delight riffs", referring to similarities with an advert for the seductively delicious chocolate bar which was being screened at the time. The song was a favourite concert piece when Barrett was in the band, and was recorded for Pink Floyd's first BBC radio session in October 1967.

FLAMING

(Barrett)
There is a childlike quality in this song also, and of course the line "here we go, ever so high" is completely innocent...

A slightly different mix was released as a single in the USA, despite the song being omitted from the first release of the album there.

Another part of the first BBC session, 'Flaming' was performed live by both the Syd

Barrett and David Gilmour line-ups, where it was sometimes sung by Roger Waters, sometimes by Gilmour. Although it didn't stay in the set list for long, it was performed in November 1969 for a French TV special, *Tous En Scène*.

 ### POW R. TOC H.
(Barrett/Waters/Wright/Mason)
"Toc H" is a charity, taking its name from army signallers' code for Talbot House, a club house just behind allied lines in World War One, where rank was ignored. Toc H aims to encourage friendships between young people from different backgrounds. Quite what all this noble activity has to do with a group-composed instrumental is not known, nor is the origin of the "Pow R." half of the title. What is known is that it was recorded for the BBC in December 1967 and survived to become known as 'The Pink Jungle', part of *The Journey*. There are some differences toward the end of the mono mix.

 ### TAKE UP THY STETHOSCOPE AND WALK
(Waters)
It is perhaps significant that the only member of the band other than Syd Barrett to have his own song used on the album was Roger

Waters, although he later described it as "a very bad song", forgetting his own advice that "music helps to ease the pain". Waters shares the vocals with Barrett, although there aren't very many of them. Indeed, the song shows little indication of the future direction of his writing.

 ### INTERSTELLAR OVERDRIVE
(Barrett/Waters/Wright/Mason)
Pink Floyd had already recorded two versions of this lengthy instrumental jam (probably the closest they came on record to the wild improvisations of their then live performances) before signing to EMI. The first was one of the tracks recorded during another, also unissued, demo recording session, the other for *Tonite Let's All Make Love In London*, detailed above. When it came to recording the track for *Piper...*, therefore, they were already quietly confident to be going out on such a radical limb.

The main theme evolved from Syd Barrett's jam around the riff from Love's 'My Little Red Book', as hummed to him by manager Peter Jenner. One persistent, if unlikely, fallacy is that the riff was lifted from the theme to the TV comedy *Steptoe And Son*.

The wild stereo panning was the work of Norman Smith, the band following the trend set by The Beatles, of working on the mono mix of the album and leaving the stereo version to studio boffins, the differences between the two versions being most noticeable at the end of the track.

A rendition for the BBC session of December 1968 showed that David Gilmour was just as capable of psychedelic wackiness as Barrett. A historic performance at the October 1969 Amougies Pop & Jazz festival, in Belgium, was honoured by Frank Zappa jamming with the band. For *The Journey* (see below), its middle section was used as 'The Labyrinths of Auximines', although the track was also performed in its own right until well into 1970. In 1971, the *Piper...* version reappeared on the *Relics* compilation.

THE GNOME
(Barrett)
Almost a straight nursery song, Syd Barrett's tale of the little folk is enhanced by Richard Wright's celesta backing – hardly a rock'n'roll instrument, but ideally suited to the task. This song, too, was recorded for the BBC in October 1967, after being used as the B-side of 'Flaming' in the US.

CHAPTER 24
(Barrett)
Both lyrics and title are derived from the *I Ching*, a 5,000 year old Chinese book of prophecies – a kind of horoscope, based on randomly thrown coins rather than astrological coincidences. The lyrics, recited over a fairly simple keyboard drone with a few lightly tickled cymbals, are virtually a rewrite of a chapter (the twenty-fourth!) which suggests new beginnings.

SCARECROW
(Barrett)
As well as being the B-side to 'See Emily Play' (the only one of the early single sides to appear on an album, compilations aside), 'Scarecrow', another nursery song, was part of the first 1967 BBC session.

BIKE
(Barrett)
Although it seems to be yet another of Syd Barrett's charming and childlike ditties, 'Bike', once planned to segue with 'Interstellar Overdrive', has a deeper significance. First, there is the very adult plea to Barrett's "girl", then the coda, a manic representation of a "room full of musical tunes", reached by footsteps like those later used to startling effect on the band's quadraphonic PA, the winding of clockwork mechanisms and finally the hauntingly oppressive chattering voices.

'Bike' was used on both the *Relics* and *Echoes* compilations.

PINK FLOYD/ 1967 – THE FIRST SINGLES

Released: 4 August 1997
as EMI 8 59895 2

A limited edition compilation, issued as a bonus with the 30th Anniversary issue of *Piper...* (see above), although some copies were reportedly sold separately. Note that each of the tracks included is a different mix or edit to those on the original vinyl singles, though all are in mono. The gatefold cardboard sleeve used the artwork from the front and back sleeves of promo copies of each single.

ARNOLD LAYNE

(Barrett)
Originally recorded at the Peter Whitehead-funded demo sessions in January 1967, this was re-recorded in the following month, at Sound Techniques with the now-legendary producer Joe Boyd (the credit reads "produced by Joe Boyd for Blackhill Enterprises"), as the band's first single (Columbia DB 8156; released 11 March 1967), reaching number 20 in the UK charts.

The song tells the tale of a clothes-stealing transvestite and was inspired by the theft of underwear from Roger Waters and Syd Barrett's female student lodgers. Such debauchery was not for pirate radio station Radio London, although the record was played by the BBC. The band, though irritated at the oversimplification of the issue, viewed this with some disinterest; since they had not wanted the single released anyway, feeling that they had progressed from such simple pop melodies.

A promo film was shot, with Barrett and the rest of the band messing around with a shop-window dummy. Waters screened this during an on stage "tea-break" during his 1987 concerts.

In later years, it appeared on the *Echoes* compilation and was performed by David Gilmour on his 2006 tour, from which it was released as a live single.

CANDY AND A CURRANT BUN

(Barrett)
First recorded at the Peter Whitehead session, when it was known as 'Let's Roll Another One', the original lyrics blatantly described the joys of soft drugs. EMI naturally balked at the idea of releasing such a ditty, and insisted both title and lyrics be changed for the B-side of 'Arnold Layne', which was also produced by Joe Boyd at Sound Techniques. Nonetheless, the "tastes good if you eat it right" line remained.

Different versions, including an outtake with no vocals, have been bootlegged.

SEE EMILY PLAY

(Barrett)
The next single, 'See Emily Play' (Columbia DB 8214; released 16 June 1967), recorded at the same time as *Piper...*, preceded the album, although Norman Smith, a producer imposed on the band by the record company, found it necessary to return to Sound Techniques to recapture the sound and spirit of 'Arnold Layne'. A visitor to the studio during the recording sessions was Syd Barrett's school friend from Cambridge, David Gilmour. 'Emily...' was promoted with three appearances on *Top Of The Pops*. Criminally, all three master tapes were erased by the BBC in the Eighties, when the storage space was needed for other programmes. Still, at least they retained their archive of football matches! Fortunately, parts of one of the recordings, from July 6, 1967, came to light in late 2009, in the possession of a private collector. At the time of writing, plans were being made for a public screening in 2010.

The song was written as 'Games For May', to mark a festival of the same name, held at the Queen Elizabeth Hall in London in May 1967. Indeed, the original title remains among the revised lyrics, although Barrett later claimed it was about a girl he saw in a wood "Up North", where he was sleeping after a concert. The real Emily was later revealed to be the Honourable Emily Young, a bona fide aristocrat, niece of the conservationist Sir Peter Scott and a regular, if under-age, visitor to the UFO Club. The song was given a few additional live performances, chiefly to appease pop fans who went to see the band on the strength of the single's position at #6 in the UK chart, and who were bewildered by the more typical instrumental jams.

A very limited number of promo copies, now much sought-after by collectors, were issued in picture sleeves, depicting a childlike drawing of a train by Barrett. His artwork was also used in press adverts for the disc.

A promo film, believed to have been shot by a Belgian TV station, has the David Gilmour-era band messing about in a park and making no attempt to mime while the studio recording plays. The film was available on a various-artist video compilation, *Rock'n'Roll Years 1967* (Video Collection VC 4058). The song resurfaced on the *Echoes* compilation.

SCARECROW
(Barrett)
'Emily's B-side was exactly the same as the version which would appear on *Piper...* It was the subject of an early – and suitably bizarre – promo film, made for a Pathe newsreel, giving the young Floyds an excuse for much cavorting and hamming.

APPLES AND ORANGES
(Barrett)
Syd Barrett's final single for the band (Columbia DB 8310; released 17 November 1967) was recorded in only two sessions, Roger Waters claiming that Norman Smith's botched production had spoiled a perfectly good song. Barrett claimed his inspiration was a girl he had seen while shopping.

It was recorded for the BBC in October 1967 and mimed by the band for their first US TV appearance, on the *Dick Clark Bandstand*, with Barrett especially seeming unwilling to co-operate. A 1968 promo video has Waters miming the vocals and David Gilmour the guitar.

Like 'Emily...', promo copies came in a picture sleeve, now hard-to-find, but with a weak design in which the band had no hand.

PAINT BOX
(Wright)
The B-side of 'Apples And Oranges' was sung by its composer. The lyrics "Sitting in a club with so many fools/Playing to the rules/Trying to impress, but feeling rather empty" give a clear indication of how he, and indeed the whole band, felt when asked to perform their pop hits instead of their preferred psychedelic improvisations.

Its descending refrain owes more than a little to The Beatles' 'A Day In The Life'. The title is written as one word, 'Paintbox', on *Relics*.

A SAUCERFUL OF SECRETS

Released 29 June 1968
as Columbia SCX 6258
UK Chart: No 9; US Chart: n/a
First CD: EMI CDP 7 46383 2
Remaster: EMI 8 29751 2; 25 July 1994

During the recording of *Saucerful...*, the one secret the band had been trying to keep from their public – the fragile state of Syd Barrett's mental health and his impending breakdown – became uncontainable. It was

originally announced that his school friend and one-time fellow busker David Gilmour would replace him for live work, with Barrett retaining responsibility for writing, but only a handful of gigs were performed as a five piece before the rest of the band simply stopped collecting Barrett on the way to gigs. One result of these changes was an album, again produced by Norman Smith, recorded under great stress by two different line-ups. Some tracks were recorded more than once, first with Barrett and then with Gilmour. Mystery has always surrounded some of these sessions, and though it is known that Barrett and Gilmour are heard together on some tracks, it is difficult to differentiate their playing – after all, Gilmour was hired partly for his ability to sound like Barrett, whom he had taught to play. During the later sessions, Barrett would sit patiently in the reception area at Abbey Road, waiting to be asked to play for "his" band. Shortly after his departure, the band ended their partnership with Peter Jenner and Andrew King (who continued to manage Barrett, and would have later success, together and separately, with a range of artists from Marc Bolan and Roy Harper to The Clash, Ian Dury and Billy Bragg). Eventually, the Floyd ended up being managed by their booking agent Steve O'Rourke, thorough his company, EMKA Productions.

The sleeve was by Storm Thorgerson (formerly a class-mate of Roger Waters and another childhood friend of Barrett and David Gilmour) and Aubrey 'Po' Powell, working as Hipgnosis, and was the first on which an EMI act, other than The Beatles, had been allowed to use an outside design team. A collage of mystical images, it has none of the panache of their later work.

Again, the mono version of the original vinyl album (Columbia SC 6258) featured different mixes, although less noticeably than on its predecessor. *Saucerful...* later formed the second part of the *A Nice Pair* vinyl reissue, alongside *Piper...*

Although the *Saucerful...* sessions began and ended at Abbey Road, some took place at Sound Techniques and De Lane Lea. These also resulted in 'Apples and Oranges' and 'Paintbox', which would end up as either side of the third single, and two as-yet unreleased tracks, 'Scream Thy Last Scream' and 'Vegetable Man'. All four are Barrett compositions and feature his singing and playing.

 ### LET THERE BE MORE LIGHT
(Waters)

This simple tale of a "close encounter of the third kind" spends its first minute demonstrating the powers of stereophonic imagery. The idea of the band as science fiction fanatics – "space rockers", indeed – was to be a millstone round their collective neck for some time, causing them much irritation. The lyrics also refer to (Pip) Carter, a friend from Cambridge who worked as one of the band's roadies.

Vocal duties fell to David Gilmour and Richard Wright – an early indication that, for the next 15 years at least, Pink Floyd's three vocalists would be used where their voices fitted best, regardless of who had written the song in question.

This was one of the numbers recorded for the band's first BBC Session with Gilmour, in August 1968. The few live performances include one for French TV's *Tous En Scène*.

 ### REMEMBER A DAY
(Wright)

Richard Wright's charming reminiscence of the simplicity of childhood is an out-take from *Piper...*, where some say it was to go under the title 'Sunshine', although there is also evidence to suggest that 'Sunshine' may have been an early version of 'Matilda Mother'. In any case, Syd Barrett plays slide guitar, although recording was finished after his departure, the vocals are by its composer and other guitar parts by David Gilmour. Norman Smith drummed and sang backing vocals, but Nick Mason is wholly absent. It was later included on *Relics*.

The song was used in the 2001 film of the same name (released on DVD in 2006 by Supersonic Films, SSF002DVD), written by the late, and legendary, Syd Barrett fan Bernard White, and which is a fictional tale about a very Barrett-like reclusive rock star. The film was directed by, and co-starred, Nigel Lesmoir-Gordon, a school-days friend of Barrett and David Gilmour. Peter Jenner played – what else – a rock manager.
A previously unreleased instrumental take of the eponymous song, personally made available to producer and star Darryl Read by Wright, was also heard, over the closing credits.

Gilmour had been due to appear on Jools Holland's live TV show *Later! Live.... with Jools Holland* on BBC2 on September 23, 2008, to promote his *Live in Gdansk* release, but Wright had died on the 15th of that month, so Gilmour and his tour band chose instead to perform 'Remember A Day', its live premiere, in his honour.

 ### SET THE CONTROLS FOR THE HEART OF THE SUN
(Waters)
Pink Floyd performed this simple, hypnotic mantra, whose title is a quote from William S. Burroughs, for their first BBC session in October 1967, obviously with Syd on guitar. He is known to have been involved in recording an early version for *Saucerful...*, but is not on the released version, which instead featured David Gilmour. That this was not clear for many years says much about the similarity of the two friends' guitar playing at the time of the hand-over. Waters claimed to have found the lyrics in a book of translated Chinese poetry.

Live versions can be found on *Ummagumma*, the Dutch video *Stamping Ground*, filmed at the Kralingen Pop Festival, of June 1970, and on *Live At Pompeii*. Pink Floyd performed lengthy renditions until the end of 1973 and 11 years later it was revamped by Roger Waters for his *Pros And Cons...* tour. It is also on *Echoes*.

 ### CORPORAL CLEGG
(Waters)
Syd, by his own admission, does not play on this early indication of Waters' scorn for the military, a theme which would become familiar to followers of the band over the next two and a half decades. The suffering war veteran of the title may have been inspired by the hero of a 1962 Hammer horror film, *Night Creatures*, one Captain Clegg. The kazoo solo is probably unique in the annals of popular music history. For which we should be thankful. Norman Smith is heard speaking on the fade out.

 ### A SAUCERFUL OF SECRETS
(Waters/Wright/Mason/Gilmour)
At the end of the recording sessions, with Syd Barrett already well out of the picture, the band's reward for compromising and recording some short pop songs was to be allowed to put down something more representative of their live show. The result was a thirteen-minute instrumental, divided into four sections, although these were not given titles until the live version was released on *Ummagumma* in 1969 – and even later copies of that album omitted to mention them. With no clear indication of where the composers considered the subdivisions to be, the following times are at best a rough guide only.

According to David Gilmour, the first part, 'Something Else', derived from a recording of a very closely miked cymbal, describes preparations for war. 'Syncopated Pandemonium' (3'59") is a Nick Mason drum pattern, recorded to tape then cut and re-spliced, over which Gilmour abuses his guitar with a microphone stand, and represents the battle itself. There is a cross-fade into 'Storm Signal' (7'02"), with more keyboard-generated noises, which is the aftermath. Finally, 'Celestial Voices' (8'39"), all sweeping organ and dreamy vocalese, which one can honestly say is quite beautiful, is thus the requiem. Live, this section would, where available, be played on the venues' pipe organs.

The structure of the piece was determined by Mason and Roger Waters – both former architecture students – who drew a series of peaks and troughs on a chart to outline its dynamics. The track paved the way for other, perhaps more structured, pieces that would evolve, via 'Atom Heart Mother' and 'Echoes', into *The Dark Side Of The Moon*.

Until corrected on the remastered CD, David Gilmour's first professional songwriting credit was misspelled 'Gilmore'.

First performed under the title 'The Massed Gadgets Of Hercules' for a BBC session in June 1968, recorded for *Ummagumma* and later seen in the *Stamping Ground* video, the 'Saucerful...' suite remained in the live set until September 1972, when it was put to rest after being filmed for *Live At Pompeii*.

SEE SAW
(Wright)
Another Richard Wright song on which Syd Barrett is believed to play, its apt working title of 'The Most Boring Song I've Ever Heard Bar Two', begs the question "What on Earth were the others?".

JUGBAND BLUES
(Barrett)
The only Syd Barrett composition, and his only vocal performance, to make it onto the second album was originally intended, at least by Peter Jenner and Andrew King, as the follow-up to the band's second single, 'See Emily Play'.

The song isn't a blues, nor is it performed by a jug-band (a forerunner of skiffle groups), although Barrett did bring members of a Salvation Army band into De Lane Lea studios to contribute to the chaotic middle section. Quite what these upright Bible-bashers made of being told to "play what you like" is probably best not thought about, but the result makes a chilling accompaniment to Barrett's schizophrenic lyrics, giving the album a very down-beat ending indeed, especially the haunting vocals after the false ending.

For the version recorded for their BBC session on the last day of December 1967, the band were without the "assistance" of William Booth's finest and had to create their own discordant middle section.

THE COMMITTEE

Released in 2005
as Basho Records EDD02056

Some time around work on *Saucerful...*, the band were asked to provide soundtrack music for a short (55-minute) black & white film, directed by Peter Sykes and starring Paul Jones, based on a short story by Max Steuer. Syd Barrett began work on the project, but did not complete it. The music – all instrumental – was therefore recorded with David Gilmour in May 1968, at around the same time that *Saucerful...* was being completed, and is typical of the band's work at that time, with heavy use of Richard Wright's electric organ. Arthur Brown, a contemporary of Pink Floyd's from the infamous UFO Club, makes an inexplicable cameo appearance in the film, performing live at the London School of Economics.

This is the only track with notable differences between the stereo and mono versions, the latter having more guitar and different vocals. In Canada, *A Nice Pair* included a different stereo mix, unknown elsewhere, while the original is on *Echoes*.

A promotional film of the song was made, for the Central Office of Information to use, promoting the UK's culture overseas. Quite what viewers made of the disintegrating Barrett's far-away look is perhaps best not imagined.

The mono soundtrack has never been released, so no track titles are known, though one sounds very like 'Careful With That Axe, Eugene'. In 2005, the film, never previously available for home use, finally made an appearance on DVD, released by Basho Records in the USA, and was described by one reviewer as being like an "introverted and intense episode of *The Twilight Zone*". The DVD includes *The Making Of The Committee*, a 51-minute retrospective filmed in 2003, comprising interviews with Sykes and Steuer. Pink Floyd are discussed from about 37 minutes in.

THE POST-BARRETT SINGLES

Though not given a proper release on CD until the 1992 *Shine On* box set, this is an appropriate point to discuss the two singles released by the band in the late 1960s, after the departure of Syd Barrett. There would be no further UK singles until 1979.

IT WOULD BE SO NICE

(Wright)
The first post-Syd single (Columbia DB 8410; released 12 April 1968) was recorded around the time the album was being completed. Sung by Wright, this was his only Floyd composition released as a single A-side, and disappeared without trace, probably because the promising, powerful intro soon descended into a novelty-song style verse, rendered listenable only by the harmonies on the rather more melodious chorus. Though they made a promotional film for the song, the band themselves soon expressed their dislike of it.

An original reference to London's *Evening Standard* newspaper had to be changed to the fictitious *Daily Standard* after complaints from the publisher. The latter version is heard here, and on all other known compilations.

JULIA DREAM

(Waters)
'It Would Be So Nice' was backed by Gilmour's vocal and guitar début for the band, in a style very similar to his singing on 'Fat Old Sun'. Although not a concert number, it was recorded for the BBC in June 1968.

The song is an early example of Waters writing about paranoia ("Will the following footsteps catch me... Am I really dying?") and there is much debate over whether Waters' whispered words in the final moments are "Syd", "Save me" or, as seems more likely, something else entirely. The early studio work was done under the title 'Doreen's Dream'.

A different version was used on the *Masters Of Rock* compilation.

POINT ME AT THE SKY

(Waters/Gilmour)
Six months after the *Saucerful...* album, Pink Floyd released their last single for 11 years (Columbia DB 8511; released 17 December 1968). Although it was never performed live, a promo film was made for 'Point Me...', featuring the band dressed in Biggles-style flying suits and cavorting with a bi-plane. The song was also filmed for *Tous En Scène* and recorded, with a minor lyric change, for the band's December 1968 BBC session. On record, Gilmour handles lead vocals, with Wright joining in and Waters singing the lyrics about "People pushing on my side..."

Lyrically, this is the strongest of the five early singles, a seemingly simple tale of an intrepid aviator soon giving way to a warning about the dangers of an overcrowded planet, perhaps an early recognition of the environmental concerns now so prevalent among successful pop stars.

CAREFUL WITH THAT AXE, EUGENE

(Waters/Wright/Gilmour/Mason)
'Point Me...'s B-side, the only early single-side drawn from the band's live set, this brooding, menacing instrumental first appeared, in 1968, as 'Murderistic Woman', (recorded for the June 1968 BBC session), later being called 'Keep Smiling People'. It also made appearances under the moniker 'Beset By Creatures Of The Deep', part of 'The Journey'. It was recorded again in May 1969, under its more familiar title, for the BBC and, at around the same time, for *Ummagumma*. Another live version, from 1971, can be seen and heard in the *Superstars In Concert* video (Telstar TVE 1003), while a different performance is in *Live At Pompeii*. Only on versions with this name is the title pronounced by Waters before the track's high-point, his scream. Another studio version, 'Come In No. 51, Your Time Is Up', was used in the film *Zabriskie Point*.

The piece had also been used among the 15 minutes of instrumental music recorded in 1968 by the band for another film soundtrack, *The Committee*, which was never fully released, although it was shown to the press. A soundtrack album was proposed at one time. Perhaps, like *Tonite Let's All Make Love In London*, the film and music master tapes are gathering dust somewhere, waiting for some keen entrepreneur to sort out contractual hassles and release them to eager fans.

Dropped from the live set in October 1973, 'Axe' was resurrected for an unexpected, one-off concert encore in Oakland, California in May 1977.

MORE

Released 27 July 1969
as Columbia SCX 6346
UK Chart: #9; US Chart: #153
First CD: EMI CDP 7 46386 2
Remaster: EMI 8 35631 2
DVD: BFI BFIVD587; 28 July 2003

Pink Floyd spent just five sessions, over eight days in February 1969, at the Pye Studios in London, putting music to director Barbet Schroeder's first feature film, which centred around drug-taking hippies in Ibiza. Some of the songs had made their live débuts some time earlier.

Quite what the freaks from the underground, who probably didn't notice David Gilmour step into Syd Barrett's shoes on *Saucerful...*, made of such a marked change in direction so early in the life of the band, no one knows, but the change was as great as any made in the rest of their career.

The album sleeve has a simple, solarised still from the film, "designed" by Hipgnosis. The full wording on the sleeve reads "Soundtrack from the film MORE played and composed by *The* Pink Floyd", using the definite article which was to prove hard for the band to shake off for the rest of their career.

As was often the case, the music heard in the cinema is very different from that re-recorded for the album. In particular, a short instrumental called 'Hollywood' and the song 'Seabirds' did not make it onto record.

The latter, heard as background music during a party scene, did feature in *The Pink Floyd Songbook* (Lupus Music/Music Sales, 1976), enabling the only known cover version, by Langford and Kerr, to appear on the *Moving Soundtracks Vol 1* compilation (Disques Du Crepuscule TWI 122-2).

The film was not judged a success, except in France, where it is held in similar regard as *Easy Rider* (the dialogue is mostly in English with some in German, Spanish and French, using English subtitles). Early home-video versions were thus released in the French SECAM format, incompatible with most other countries' systems. In 2003 the 111-minute film was released on DVD by the British Film Institute (BFI), with extra features including the text of a 1969 interview with Schroeder (which makes no mention of Pink Floyd), and the film's original trailer, but sadly with only a lo-fi mono soundtrack. The opening credits list the band members, including one "dave gilmore".

CIRRUS MINOR
(Waters)
Named after a type of cloud formation, this opens with a library recording of bird song (including a common cuckoo, but most prominently a song thrush), descriptively labelled "Dawn Chorus", followed by Richard Wright's over-dubbed Hammond and Farfisa organ tracks and a few gentle vocal lines from David Gilmour.

The recording session for this song was featured in a BBC Radio Three documentary *Laying Down Tracks*.

THE NILE SONG
(Waters)
In which Pink Floyd go heavy metal, Gilmour's shouted vocals contrasting starkly with those in the preceding number. Its strength impressed sufficiently to warrant release as a single in Europe (but not the UK), Japan and New Zealand.

CRYING SONG
(Waters)
The album switches back to lullaby mode just as quickly, adding a laid-back, jazzy feel courtesy of Roger Waters' mellow bass riff.

The lyric "Help me roll away the stone" is Waters' first use of an image that would resurface on 'Animals' and 'The Wall'.

UP THE KHYBER
(Mason/Wright)
The only writing collaboration by its authors in the band's history is a two-minute instrumental, with Mason's hypnotic drumming complemented by Richard Wright's avant-garde piano stabs and choppy organ riffs.

The title, worthy of the "Carry On" team at their most risqué, refers to the hippies' associations with the Khyber Pass, which

links Pakistan with Afghanistan, and has been the scene of both mystic aspirations and military tension for many years, being the route used by many invaders of (what was once) India, including Persians, Greeks, Tartars, Mughals, Alexander the Great and the British, who turned it into a key border post during the occupation of India.

GREEN IS THE COLOUR
(Waters)
A blend of tin whistle, upright piano and Gilmour's almost whispered vocals give this lyrically obscure song a charming, folksy feel.

Used as the first part of 'The Journey', imaginatively titled 'The Beginning', it was segued into 'Careful With That Axe, Eugene'. This pairing was recorded for the band's last studio session for BBC Radio One, in May 1969, some time before the sessions for the film soundtrack, performed for the 1970 *In Concert* broadcast, and remained together in the live set until dropped in mid- 1971, to make way for 'Echoes'.

CYMBALINE
(Waters)
With lyrics such as "will the final couplet rhyme?" (it doesn't!) and "your manager and agent are both busy on the phone/selling colour photographs to magazines back home", Roger Waters was, perhaps, beginning to respond to the pressures inherent in the industry of which he was forced to be part, in order to carry out his craft. The theme would be repeated many, many times throughout his career, and was further evidenced by the song's title when it was performed as part of *The Man* – 'Nightmare'.

The title may be borrowed from Shakespeare's play *Cymbeline*, although why this should be so is not apparent. Richard Wright produces another of his "Turkish Delight" organ solos and, although Waters handled the lyrics for the version heard in the film, David Gilmour sings a slightly rewritten version of them for the album.

Another feature of the May 1969 BBC session, 'Cymbaline' became something of a live favourite, the band often performing very lengthy versions until it was demoted from the set-list at the end of 1971.

PARTY SEQUENCE
(Waters/Wright/Gilmour/Mason)
This brief instrumental consists of some vaguely Arabic-sounding reed instrument, played over Nick Mason's frantic drum pattern.

MAIN THEME
(Waters/Wright/Gilmour/Mason)
The introductory cymbal-tickling is as likely to be Roger Waters' work as Nick Mason's, as it was one of his favourite on-stage pastimes at that time. Soon the track settles into one of his trademark repetitive bass riffs, over which Richard Wright's organ, Mason's drums, a small dose of guitar and synthesiser washes discreetly mingle. Briefly included in the live set during 1970, the tune was extended to fourteen minutes on one memorable occasion. Mason is denied his credit on the CD issue.

IBIZA BAR
(Waters/Wright/Gilmour/Mason)
Same tune as 'The Nile Song', performed in a slightly (but only just) lighter mood.

MORE BLUES
(Waters/Wright/Gilmour/Mason)
This really is a blues, suggesting, whatever the credit, that Gilmour played a key part in its composition.

QUICKSILVER
(Waters/Wright/Gilmour/Mason)
A shimmering instrumental which also formed the basis of 'Sleeping', part of *The Man*. Some of the electronic sounds used are reminiscent of 'On The Run' from *Dark Side*....

A SPANISH PIECE
(Gilmour)
In the film, this was heard coming from a radio in a bar. The cod-Spanish

spoken parts (sounding like *Fawlty Towers'* Manuel on a bad trip) are, in reality, Pink Floyd's David Gilmour having a bad idea.

DRAMATIC THEME

(Waters/Wright/Gilmour/Mason)
Another short instrumental, incorrectly credited to just Roger Waters and Richard Wright on the CD version, with David Gilmour's guitar beginning to soar as his inimitable style made its first, tentative appearance on record.

THE MASSED GADGETS OF AUXIMINES

Live performances only

At this point in the Pink Floyd story, it is useful to clarify a characteristic of their 1969 concerts. Under the generic title *The Massed Gadgets Of Auximines*, they performed two suites, *The Man* and *The Journey*, each roughly the length of an album side and comprising a number of pieces, some of which were more familiar under other names, some of which were new, and which were never recorded in their own right. Although the idea of recording them as an album was abandoned because so much of the material was borrowed from earlier records, these suites can clearly be seen as the forerunners of 'Atom Heart Mother', 'Echoes' and *The Dark Side Of The Moon*. Composer credits for some of the numbers can be deduced by reference to their album equivalents.

The Man was made up of:

DAYBREAK

A band performance of 'Grantchester Meadows'.

WORK

During the piece, according to a bootlegged Dutch radio broadcast, the band performed a little carpentry on stage. A very jazzy tune, it also featured a trombone solo by Richard Wright, and David Gilmour's very "heavy metal" guitar solo. The studio version, 'Biding My Time', has only ever been released on *Relics*.

AFTERNOON

A break for the band, with roadies serving tea on stage. Roger Waters repeated this exercise on his solo tours.

DOING IT!

A short drum solo.

SLEEPING

A predominantly keyboard instrumental, similar to 'Quicksilver'. During its introduction, a tape of breathing sounds, the band members apparently "slept" on stage.

NIGHTMARE

'Cymbaline'.

DAYBREAK

An instrumental reprise.

The Journey was:

THE BEGINNING

'Green Is The Colour', which segued into...

BESET BY CREATURES OF THE DEEP

'Careful With That Axe, Eugene'.

THE NARROW WAY

A band version of what was to become Part 3 of David Gilmour's solo contribution to 'Ummagumma'.

THE PINK JUNGLE
'Pow R. Toc H.'

THE LABYRINTHS
OF AUXIMINES
An instrumental, based on the middle section of 'Interstellar Overdrive'.

BEHOLD THE TEMPLE
OF LIGHT
Another instrumental.

THE END OF THE BEGINNING
The 'Celestial Voices' part of 'A Saucerful Of Secrets'.

UMMAGUMMA

Released 25 October 1969
as Harvest SHDW 1/2
UK Chart: #5; US Chart: #74
First CD: EMI CDS 7 46404 8
Remaster: EMI 8 31202 2

Released just three months after *More*, *Ummagumma* took its unlikely name from a slang word for sex. Pink Floyd had moved sideways from one EMI subsidiary label to another, new, one, Harvest, intended by its founder, Malcolm Jones, to capture the spirit of the new, progressive underground music. Harvest took the brave step of allowing the band to combine a straightforward live album with a second disc, comprising four sections, each recorded by one band member as a solo activity, guided, for the last time, by a bemused Norman Smith. This was Harvest's first ever double album, and the first record on the label to chart. The studio sessions coincided with those for Syd Barrett's first solo album, *The Madcap Laughs*, which Gilmour and Waters partly produced.

The live sides, produced by the band, were recorded at two concerts, the first at Birmingham's legendary Mothers Club on April 27, 1969, the other on May 2 at the Chamber of Commerce, Manchester. Radio One DJ John Peel, at whose wedding Nick Mason was best man, once described the burglary of his flat, where the only item stolen was an acetate copy of a recording of 'Interstellar Overdrive', then under consideration for inclusion on the album.

Aside from 'Grantchester Meadows', and perhaps the final part of 'The Narrow Way', the solo sides are a brave experiment that fails, or at least has dated badly, and although the various pieces are interesting on first hearing, they certainly don't bear repeated listening. All in all, it's a shame that Pink Floyd didn't opt for a more conventional double live album, perhaps recording *The Man* and *The Journey* in their entirety. It has been suggested that the subdivision of three of the solo contributions and 'Saucerful...' may have more to do with ensuring the fair division of royalties than purely musical considerations.

Hipgnosis' intriguing design for the album included the sleeve of the cast recording of the musical *Gigi*, which was subsequently airbrushed from US versions – perhaps because of copyright problems. The rear sleeve depicted the band's roadies (one of whom is Alan Stiles, later immortalised in 'Alan's Psychedelic Breakfast') and equipment, spread-eagled on a runway at Biggin Hill airfield in the style of a weaponry display. Inside the gatefold sleeve, Roger Waters was pictured with his first wife, Jude. For the first CD booklet, she was discreetly omitted, as was the Biggin Hill shot.

The first track recorded for the album, and never completed, was a group composition, 'Embryo'. The band were horrified when it was included on a compilation of Harvest material, *Picnic* (Harvest SHSS 1/2), which they insisted be withdrawn immediately. Despite this, 'Embryo' was performed live on many occasions up until the end of 1971,

having first appeared in the BBC session recorded in December 1968, and can still be obtained on the *Works* compilation CD in the USA.

The remastered *Ummagumma* was the most radical of the 1994 repackaging exercises, being presented as two separate discs (Live: 8 31213 2; Studio: 8 31214 2) in an embossed card slipcase, with a fold-out poster of the album cover. The Biggin Hill shot was resurrected, joined by several new shots from that session, but the individual band portraits were all different to the originals. Jude remained absent and the new in-concert shots dated from 1974 or after. The studio disc listed the lyrics for 'Grantchester Meadows', but not 'The Narrow Way Part 3'.

ASTRONOMY DOMINE
(Barrett)
Gilmour proved himself perfectly capable of stepping into Barrett's shoes, even on one of the latter's trademark pieces, just as he would do again in 1994. A short organ solo is the only noticeable variation from the original.

CAREFUL WITH THAT AXE, EUGENE
(Waters/Wright/Gilmour/Mason)
A splendid rendition of a concert favourite which had previously been available to record buyers only as the B-side to Pink Floyd's fifth (and, until 1979, last) single, 'Point Me At The Sky'. Always better live than on record, Waters' scream could be as chilling as anything ever heard in a Hammer Horror film.

SET THE CONTROLS FOR THE HEART OF THE SUN
(Waters)
Although almost double the length, this is not dissimilar to the original version on *Saucerful...*, the extra time being accounted for merely by a slower tempo, a meandering middle section of no great merit, and more of Richard Wright's "Turkish Delight" organ.

A SAUCERFUL OF SECRETS
(Waters/Wright/Mason/Gilmour)
Labels on original copies of *Ummagumma*, at least in the USA, gave four subdivisions: 'Something Else'; 'Syncopated Pandemonium'; 'Storm Signal' and 'Celestial Voices', although these titles are omitted from later vinyl pressings and the CD release. They are explained in more detail under the studio version's entry.

SYSYPHUS (PARTS 1-4)
(Wright)
Richard Wright's instrumental contribution to the second half of the album was named after a character in Greek mythology, more usually spelt "Sisyphus", the King who built Corinth and was condemned, in Hades, the underworld, to forever roll a huge stone ball up a hill, only for it to roll back down again (a feeling not unlike trying to unravel Pink Floyd's early history). His crime was to trap Thanatos, the god of death, thereby evading his own end and meaning that no one else could die.

Part 1 is mystical synthesiser with timpani, while, in places, Part 2 could easily be taken for a romantic-era classical piano sonata, although this image is soon dissipated by Wright's deliberate use of atonal keyboard runs. Part 3 is very experimental, but has little else to recommend it, and Part 4, opening with birdsong, relies heavily on Wright's Mellotron, eventually returning to the theme of Part 1.

Very few audiences were treated to hearing 'Sysyphus' live, though it was included at a notable gig at Birmingham Town Hall in February 1970, when the band were forced to perform an ad-hoc set after the non-arrival of a truckload of equipment. A short segment of televised studio performance, reputedly for the BBC's popular science show *Tomorrow's World*, has also been bootlegged.

GRANTCHESTER MEADOWS
(Waters)
Opening with yet morebird song, the first of Roger Waters' two contributions is a simple song about the beautiful, unspoilt area of Cambridge where he, and other future Floyds, frolicked in their youth (David Gilmour was keen on swimming in the nearby River Cam). His tale of larks, foxes and kingfishers perfectly captures the essence of the English countryside in summer. The song segues into the next piece with a fly buzzing between speakers, Waters finally dispatching it with what one assumes is a rolled up copy of an uncomplimentary review.

A band version was performed as 'Daybreak', part of *The Man,* Richard Wright's organ playing being particularly prominent. As 'Daybreak', it was recorded for the May 1969 BBC session, using piano instead of organ.

SEVERAL SPECIES OF SMALL FURRY ANIMALS GATHERED TOGETHER IN A CAVE AND GROOVING WITH A PICT
(Waters)
Waters' other contribution, later parodied in 'To Roger Waters Wherever You Are', by Ron Geesin on his *As He Stands* album, is a different matter entirely, comprising a variety of tape loops played at different speeds and in different directions. In the days of LP records, it was possible, by destroying one's copy and stylus, to discern such oddities as Waters repeating "Bring back my guitar", saying "That was pretty avant-garde, wasn't it", drumming his hands on a table and ending with an almost inaudible "Thank you" in the left-hand channel. At the right speed, he is heard ranting bad poetry, improvised on the spot, in an even worse Scottish accent. Sadly, one of the few disadvantages of compact discs is that the joys of this kind of vinyl abuse are lost to a new generation of Floyd followers. Contrary to oft-repeated rumours, Geesin played no part in the track.

Fortunately for concert goers, the track was never heard live, although Waters' "ranting Scotsman" did surface occasionally during extended performances of 'Embryo' and other pieces.

THE NARROW WAY (PARTS 1-3)
(Gilmour)

Parts 1 and 2 are both instrumental, the former being acoustic guitar with over-dubbed glissandos and high-pitched notes on an electric, the second a much heavier mêlée of electronically treated guitars which segue, via a sustained Moog note, into the third part, a rather pleasant song on which Gilmour was able to demonstrate his talent as a drummer.

Gilmour found great difficulty in writing the lyrics and requested help from Waters, which was refused. His problems were, perhaps, a portent of the dilemma he would find himself in once he assumed leadership of the band.

Part 1 was performed as 'Baby Blue Shuffle In D Major' during the December 1968 BBC Session and Part 3, under its own name, as part of *The Journey*, a band effort which in turn was recorded for the BBC in May 1969.

THE GRAND VIZIER'S GARDEN PARTY (PART 1 ENTRANCE; PART 2 ENTERTAINMENT; PART 3 EXIT)
(Mason)

It is probable that Mason cheated for Parts One and Three, calling on his then-wife, Lindy, to play the same short flute tune for both. Lindy was an accomplished flautist, for whom Ron Geesin wrote music.

Part 2 is a series of percussion exercises, some treated electronically, which, like the majority of solo drum recordings, go on far, far too long, but not as long as the Turkish Empire, where the Grand Vizier was a senior official.

ZABRISKIE POINT

Released March 1970
as MGM 2315 002
Did not chart
First CD: EMI CDP 7 94217 2
Reissue: EMI 8 23364 2

Pink Floyd's third major soundtrack project, for Michelangelo Antonioni, didn't go as well as the first two. After two weeks in the studio, in November and December 1969, much of their work was rejected for being "Too sad" or "Too strong". Eventually, Antonioni substituted tracks by The Grateful Dead and such legendary superstars as Roscoe Holcomb and John Fahey. He did use four pieces, three of which are shorter than, and differ from, the versions released on the soundtrack album. The fourth, an untitled instrumental, lasting about one minute, isn't on the album at all.

Though widely bootlegged – often with poor quality – the film has never had a DVD release and is no longer available on video tape. A laserdisc version was released in the USA (MGM /UA 100196, reissued as MGM /UA 105730).

In 1997, EMI released a double CD version, including a second disc of outtakes: four "Love Scene" improvisations by Gerry Garcia, totalling over half an hour, and two for the same scene, plus two new songs, by Pink Floyd. David Fricke provided impressively illuminating notes for the accompanying booklet, spoiled only by the frustration they

cause in their mouth-watering description of further outtakes. Apparently, an amount of material equal again in length to the new material remains in the vaults. Some tracks have been bootlegged, although the titles by which they have become known, including 'Oneone' and 'Fingal's Cave', may be the inventions of bootleggers, rather than the band themselves.

One of the unused pieces, 'The Violent Sequence', intended to accompany a scene depicting riots at the University of California in Los Angeles, with emphasis on the brutality of the police, would resurface on *Dark Side....* The version recorded for the film is heard in brief on *The Making of The Dark Side...* DVD.

HEAT BEAT, PIG MEAT
(Waters/Gilmour/Mason/Wright)
An organ and drums based instrumental, written for the opening credits. Some dialogue is heard on the released version, as is a snatch of classical string music.

CRUMBLING LAND
(Waters/Gilmour/Mason/Wright)
This is longer than the version heard in the film, but an even longer take

has been bootlegged. The vocals, shared by David Gilmour and Richard Wright, seem to relate to the plot of the film.

COME IN NO. 51, YOUR TIME IS UP
(Waters/Gilmour/Mason/Wright)
Yet another remake of 'Careful With That Axe, Eugene', this is used at the end of the film, to accompany slow-motion images of a building exploding. The scream is one of Waters' best.

COUNTRY SONG
(Waters/Gilmour/Mason/Wright)
The band's playful dynamics are shown well here with alternating verses in pastoral and heavy styles, all sung by David Gilmour. The rather unusual lyrics, describing a chess game between the Red Queen and White King, which ends in peace as the queen has every piece painted pink, seem to owe a lot to Lewis Carroll, if not to something he might have imbibed.

UNKNOWN SONG
(Waters/Gilmour/Mason/Wright)
Perhaps "Unknown Lyrics" would have been a better title, as this is, in fact, a guitar-driven instrumental, previously bootlegged under the title 'Rain In The

Country'. The way it has fades at beginning and end suggests that it may have been part of a longer improvisation. One of the bass riffs was later reused in 'Atom Heart Mother'.

LOVE SCENE VERSION 6
(Waters/Gilmour/Mason/Wright)
A competent, enjoyable, but unremarkable blues jam, lasting over seven minutes, and bearing little relation – other than a shared heritage – to anything else in the Pink Floyd canon.

LOVE SCENE VERSION 4
(Waters/Gilmour/Mason/Wright)
A solo piano piece by Richard Wright (the full-band writing credit is presumably a formality), this has nothing at all in common with Version 6 nor, again, anything else by Pink Floyd. File under "lounge music".

ATOM HEART MOTHER

Released 10 October 1970
as Harvest SHVL 781
UK Chart: #1; US Chart No. 55
First: CD EMI CDP 7 46381 2
Remaster: EMI 8 31246 2

Produced by "The" Pink Floyd (that troublesome definite article again, dropped for the CD booklets), at Abbey Road, with Alan Parsons credited as one of the studio engineers and Norman Smith "promoted" to executive producer, *Atom Heart Mother* was the Harvest label's first British Number one. It is difficult to imagine such a radical piece

of music topping the charts these days, or indeed ever again.

Atom Heart Mother was the first Pink Floyd album to be released (as Harvest Q4SHVL 781) for the new quadraphonic, or four-speaker system; a particularly appropriate move, since they had been using quadraphonic, and even six-way, sound in their concerts since 1969. Indeed, they still use a four-way split to this day.

The cover is now better known than the music within, starring a bemused looking, and deliberately bemusing, cow (named "Lulubelle III", if you must know), photographed by Hipgnosis with the specific intention of having a cover which had no meaning, and was not related in any way to the music. Further cow photographs were added to the 1994 reissue, which also offers much crisper sound.

ATOM HEART MOTHER (FATHER'S SHOUT; BREAST MILKY; MOTHER FORE; FUNKY DUNG; MIND YOUR THROATS PLEASE; REMERGENCE)

(Mason/Gilmour/Waters/Wright/Geesin)
The album's side-long title track was orchestrated and co-composed by Ron Geesin, with whom Waters had already recorded a film soundtrack, *The Body*. He was handed rough tapes by the band who, with only a few pointers, asked him to overdub "something grand". Geesin used the cello player from *The Body*, ten brass players and twenty-strong choir. When the politics of working with so many session players (classical musicians are notoriously difficult in such circumstances) proved too much for him, choir leader John Aldiss took over from Geesin as conductor. Geesin still considers the released version to be little better than a demo and wanted at the time to re-record the piece. As, indeed, did the band, but time and funds forbade such a luxury.

Its début performance was in Paris in February 1970 (did this really come just three years after 'Arnold Layne'?). Later, at their Bath Festival appearance in June of that year, Roger Waters introduced the première of the "orchestral" version, which a disappointed Ron Geesin left mid-performance, as 'The Amazing Pudding'. It did not gain its familiar title until it was performed, in September 1970, at the BBC's Paris Theatre, for an *In Concert* broadcast. Asked for a title for the programme's log sheet, the band hurriedly scanned a newspaper, eventually finding a story headlined "Nuclear drive for woman's heart" about a woman with a new kind of pacemaker.

Further live performances followed, both with and without an accompanying orchestra and choir, lasting anything from fourteen to thirty minutes, and the piece led to Pink Floyd being the first and only rock band to perform at the prestigious Montreux festival of classical music.

For the curious, the various parts begin at 5'19", 10'09", 15'25", 17'44" and 19'45", although they are not indexed individually on the 1994 CD, as they were on the first version, at least for listeners with equipment capable of reading such subdivisions.

IF
(Waters)
The deceptive simplicity of the opening lines and uncomplicated, acoustic guitar do not prepare the listener for the sudden switch to references to insanity and loneliness. It was an early sign to those in the know that Syd's influence – or, more specifically, guilt over his departure – would stay with Waters for a while yet.

Although the band never performed 'If' live (except as part of the above-mentioned BBC *In Concert* show), it was released as a single in the US and mainland Europe. In the Eighties, Roger Waters revived it for his *Pros And Cons* and *Radio KAOS* tours.

SUMMER '68
(Wright)
Although Richard Wright claims never to have been happy as a lyric writer, he does concede that this song, questioning a casual pick-up or possibly a groupie (its working title was 'One Night Stand'), embodies his own true feelings. Even so, it is the only track on the album never to have been played live.

The "brass" interlude is played on an early synthesiser, with Wright singing the verses and Gilmour the heavier choruses.

FAT OLD SUN
(Gilmour)
David Gilmour wrote this very English song as a sequel to 'Grantchester Meadows' and played everything on it, except Richard Wright's keyboard part. From the opening church bells to the gentle acoustic guitar and muted drums, it is a perfect vehicle for the most mellow singing of his career. It was recorded for two BBC *In Concert* shows, the 1970 one referred to

already, and one in October 1971, as well as becoming a regular part of the 1970 and '71 live sets, and being played by Gilmour on his 2006 tour.

Poignantly, this was also the song that Gilmour, Nick Mason and Richard Wright performed in November 2003, playing together for the first time since 1994, at the Chichester Cathedral funeral of their long-time friend and manager Steve O'Rourke.

 ALAN'S PSYCHEDELIC BREAKFAST (RISE AND SHINE; SUNNY SIDE UP; MORNING GLORY)
(Waters/Mason/Gilmour/Wright)
Thirteen minutes of tomfoolery, named after Pink Floyd roadie Alan Stiles, whose voice can be heard as he performs his morning ritual. One of its keyboard riffs would later reappear as the basis of 'Profiles', the title track of Nick Mason's second solo album.

Between musical passages, Stiles is heard washing himself and frying bacon. Such *musique concrète*, or non-musical sound, was to become a hallmark of almost every Pink Floyd album, not to mention Roger Waters' solo work, but none would use it as much as this piece, which was performed live, unsurprisingly, only a handful of times, in December 1970. During the performance, the band brewed tea and cooked on stage.

The dripping tap which closes the piece originally continued, *ad infinitum*, in the vinyl album's run-out groove. The track's subdivisions are at 4'29" and 8'18" on the original CD issue.

RELICS

Released 14 May 1971
as Starline SRS 5071
UK Chart: #32; US Chart: #152
Remaster: EMI 8 356030 2;
9 March 1996
UK Chart: #48 (1996 reissue)

Tracks: Arnold Layne; Interstellar Overdrive; See Emily Play; Remember A Day; Paintbox; Julia Dream; Careful With That Axe, Eugene; Cirrus Minor; The Nile Song; Biding My Time; Bike.

Following the chart success of *Atom Heart Mother*, EMI's budget-price subsidiary Starline released this compilation of early singles, album tracks and one new piece. The sleeve is graced by Nick Mason's pen and ink drawing – shaded pink on later releases – of a strange machine, with its subtitle, "A Bizarre Collection of Antiques and Curios". Overseas, two alternative covers have been used. Australia's showed old Spanish coins, while in America a grotesque bottle opener, fashioned to represent a head with two pairs of eyes, was depicted. The Japanese version had a gatefold sleeve with Mason's drawing.

EMI Australia briefly released *Relics* on CD (EMI CDAX 701290). This reportedly occurred without the band's consent, hence its rapid withdrawal.

In the mid 1990s, EMI considered an updated CD version, with added rarities,

but this did not come to pass, and the eventually authorised CD release, in 1996, reused only the original contents, albeit remastered by James Guthrie and Doug Sax. It did, though, have a snazzy new cover, and a booklet, using photographs of a model of the weird device drawn by Mason, and different versions of his drawings. The model was later seen gracing the offices of Mason's motor-racing company.

The album included one otherwise unreleased song:

 BIDING MY TIME
(Waters)
Only ever played live a handful of times in its own right, this also appeared as 'Work' in *The Man* suite. The trombone is played by Richard Wright. Recording took place at Abbey Road in July 1969, shortly after the end of sessions for *Ummagumma*.

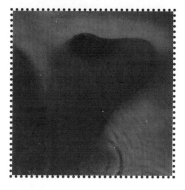

MEDDLE

Released 13 November 1971
as Harvest SHVL 795
UK Chart: #3; US Chart: #70
First CD: Harvest CDP 7 46034 2
Remaster: EMI 8 29749 2;
1 August 1994

Regarded by many as the album where the band first showed its mettle – no doubt a reflection of David Gilmour's growing confidence – *Meddle* comprises two tone poems and four fairly standard songs, produced by the band at Air Studios (the band's first 16-track sessions), Abbey Road, Morgan Sound and Richard Wright's kitchen.

Work was said to have been done on a quadraphonic mix, but if this exists, it has never seen the light of day.

The sleeve is another Hipgnosis creation: a pig's ear, under rippling water, representing the echoes of the lead track – ideal for a band for whom sonic qualities have often been as important as tunes and words.

ONE OF THESE DAYS
(Mason/Gilmour/Waters/Wright)
In the *Live At Pompeii* film – and often at concerts – this was referred to by its full, somewhat unfriendly title, 'One Of These Days, I'm Going To Cut You Into Little Pieces', as declaimed by Nick Mason's solitary, slowed down, vocal contribution.

The opening wind gives way to a menacing bass riff (courtesy of a device called a Binson echo unit) which itself precedes staccato keyboards and solid, if unadventurous, drumming, before some convincing slide guitar. The bass guitar is double tracked, with Gilmour playing on one stereo channel and Waters following on the other. The naggingly familiar tune just after the three-minute mark is a light-hearted snatch of the theme to television favourite *Doctor Who*.

Always a live favourite, it was included in the BBC *In Concert* show of October 1971, the last time they performed specifically for the BBC (the recording also included a blues instrumental, which has only ever been broadcast in the US). It opened the second set on the 1987-88 tour, while nightly performances in 1994 yielded a live version for the B-side of the 'High Hopes'/'Keep Talking' single.

In *Live At Pompeii*, Gilmour plays the piece on his usual Stratocaster, but for more recent live performances, he has preferred a pedal steel guitar, as can clearly be seen in the *Delicate Sound Of Thunder* video. The track is the oldest on the *...Great Dance Songs* collection, and an abridged version of the studio version is on *Echoes*.

A PILLOW OF WINDS
(Gilmour/Waters)
More pastoral, dreamy Englishness, held together by Richard Wright's organ, despite its low place in the mix. Like 'Fearless' and 'San Tropez', this never warranted a live performance, suggesting that they were seen by the band, to some degree, as filler. The title is from a scoring combination in the game mahjong.

FEARLESS
(Gilmour/Waters)
Unremarkable, although Roger Waters' lyrics, sung by David Gilmour over the latter's tune, hint at things to come. The coda is an a cappella rendition of Rodgers & Hammerstein's 'You'll Never Walk Alone' recorded at the Kop end of Liverpool F.C.'s Anfield ground, where it was the crowd's anthem.

SAN TROPEZ
(Waters)
A jazzy little number with emphasis on Richard Wright's piano. David Gilmour's unexpected Hawaiian guitar middle eight is unfamiliar territory, but still manages to demonstrate his virtuosity.

SEAMUS
(Mason/Gilmour/Waters/Wright)
A canine throwaway, it's a pity a better vehicle has never been found for Gilmour's authentic-sounding bluegrass guitar work. The track came about after the band discovered that their friend and fellow musician Steve Marriott owned a dog, Seamus, which would howl to music.

The piece was performed for the *Live at Pompeii* film, under the title 'Mademoiselle Nobs', the track's only "live" outing, taking its title from another canine soloist, the pet of concert promoter Claude Nobs, founder of the Montreux Jazz Festival and the "Funky Claude" referred to in Deep Purple's 'Smoke On The Water' – perhaps Seamus's rider was too demanding?

ECHOES
(Mason/Gilmour/Waters/Wright)
The band filled the second side of the album with a twenty-three and a half minute masterpiece, composed by linking together twenty-odd short riffs and themes, in turn the results of studio jamming with tapes running. They were given the working title of 'Nothing, Parts 1-24'. As the work progressed, tapes were labelled, in the style of a Japanese monster movie, 'Son Of Nothing' and 'The Return Of The Son Of Nothing', a mundane explanation of the rather mystical-sounding name sometimes given to the track by bootleggers. The lyrics of early performances made reference to planets and space, but by the time of its release, the message had become more inward looking. Waters has described them as the beginning of the empathic tone which has been part of his work ever since.

The opening "sonar" ping was discovered by accident when Richard Wright fed his piano through a Leslie amplifier. Much time was later expended trying to recapture the exact sound, but when this proved impossible, the effect had to be edited from one of the original demos, recorded at Abbey Road. Other than that, 'Echoes' was recorded entirely at Air Studios.

The tension in the crescendo leading up to the third verse is truly awesome, but the verse itself is no anticlimax, more a post-coital glow. Listening to live tapes, one could sympathise with an audience that never wanted the music to end.

'Echoes' was used to good effect in the film *Pink Floyd – Live At Pompeii* where it was performed, in two parts, book-ending the concert with no audience. It was also the highlight of the band's 1971 BBC *In Concert* recording. Another performance was recorded by the BBC in 1974, at the same time as the *Dark Side...* concert. Apparently, it's absolutely wonderful, but the band has always refused to allow it to be broadcast. The 1971 concert recording also included a blues instrumental, but this has only ever been broadcast once, in the USA.

The middle passage of 'Echoes' was occasionally borrowed for live performances of 'Embryo'. To best understand how this section was recorded, budding guitar superstars should watch Gilmour's performance in *Live At Pompeii*.

Despite their growing live success, Roger Waters sometimes expressed his boredom during concerts by introducing the piece with silly names. 'Looking Through The Knotholes In Granny's Wooden Leg' was one, as was 'We Won The Double', after his football team, Arsenal, won both the league title and FA Cup in 1971. 'The March Of The Dambusters' might also have been funny, had Pink Floyd not been playing in Germany at the time!

The studio recording of 'Echoes' also featured in a lengthy sequence of the surfing film *Crystal Voyager* (DVD released on Blue Dolphin Film and Video in March 2003, extras include an interview with director David Elfick, which discusses Pink Floyd's involvement), where it accompanies scenes shot by a surfboard-mounted camera with waves breaking all around. This obviously impressed the band, as they came to an arrangement with the film's surfer and cameraman, George Greenough, to use the footage when the track, and later 'Great Gig In The Sky', was performed live. In the early 1990s, an advertising agency attempted to obtain clearance to use 'Echoes' and the Crystal Voyager footage to promote a toilet cleaner. They were, unsurprisingly, unsuccessful.

There were a few renditions of 'Echoes' on the opening handful of dates of Pink Floyd's 1987 tour. Sadly, it was dropped all too soon, Gilmour apparently feeling uncomfortable with its "hippy" lyrics. Nonetheless, he resurrected it for his 2006 tour, and a live version will be on his *Remember That Night* DVD. A heavily abridged version of the studio original is on the *Echoes* compilation, to which it gave its name.

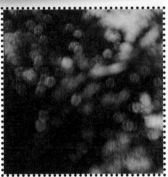

The cover shot is a deliberately out of focus still from the film, lacking any of the cleverness one would expect of Hipgnosis.

Very much overlooked by casual fans, of all the band's creations this is justifiably one of Nick Mason's favourites.

Although not yet available on DVD in the UK, the 105-minute film was released in the USA in February 2003 (Home Vision Entertainment VAL30) with the original mono soundtrack, English subtitles and an uncorrected tear in the print. There are no extra features.

OBSCURED BY CLOUDS
(Waters/Gilmour)
A pulsing instrumental, whose opening synthesiser riff was blatantly ripped off for an aftershave advert in the Eighties.

WHEN YOU'RE IN
(Waters/Gilmour/Mason/Wright)
Very similar to the preceding track, but with more prominent drums, the two being performed as one number late in 1972 and throughout 1973.

BURNING BRIDGES
(Wright/Waters)
Sung by David Gilmour and Richard Wright, this otherwise insignificant little ballad is made memorable by neat guitar work, which has very little in common with Gilmour's work on subsequent albums. It is one of only three joint compositions by Wright and Roger Waters, the others being 'Stay' and 'Us And Them'.

THE GOLD IT'S IN THE...
(Waters/Gilmour)
This raucous rocker, sung by Gilmour, benefits from the rawness forced on the band by the short deadlines to which they were working, and puts to death the myth that they were nothing without studio trickery.

OBSCURED BY CLOUDS

Released: 3 June 1972
as Harvest SHSP 4020
UK Chart: #6; US Chart: #46
First CD: EMI CDP 7 46385 2

Produced by Pink Floyd in less than two weeks, at the famous Château d'Herouville near Paris (immortalised by Elton John in *Honky Château*), this is the soundtrack to the movie *La Vallée* (also known as *Obscured By Clouds*), by *More* director Barbet Schroeder. The film, whose dialogue is in French, tells the tale of a bunch of hippies going native as they search for a lost valley in New Guinea.

Like *More,* the music on the album is different from the short extracts heard in the film, and features Pink Floyd's first use of the VCS3 synthesiser.

WOT'S... UH THE DEAL
(Waters/Gilmour)

For the first half of this song, David Gilmour sings over some simple acoustic guitar, later joined by drums and bass. Richard Wright then contributes a piano solo before Gilmour responds with electric guitar. Despite its lack of Pink Floyd trademarks, the very simplicity of the song makes it the album's unexpected treasure. But why is there a four-note organ riff in the fade out? Even more unexpected was Gilmour's use of this song on his 2006 tour, when it had never been performed live by Pink Floyd.

MUDMEN
(Wright/ Gilmour)

Until 'Cluster One' on *The Division Bell*, this was the only track in Pink Floyd's history on which Richard Wright and David Gilmour shared full writing credits. 'Mudmen' is an instrumental vehicle for swirling organ and layers of guitar, including two solos which mark the birth of the style that Gilmour would milk so successfully during the late Seventies and Eighties, both for Floyd albums and during his many guest sessions for other artists.

CHILDHOOD'S END
(Gilmour)

Other than the contentious first track on *Dark Side...*, this was to be the last song recorded by Pink Floyd without Roger Waters' name attached to it, and David Gilmour's last lyric, for the rest of Waters' time with the band. It has been suggested that the title came from the book of the same name by Arthur C. Clarke.

This is very much the composer's track, although his vocals and intense guitar are ably supported by Wright's organ and Mason's drumming, earning it a handful of live performances in late 1972 and early '73. The strict-tempo drum pattern laid down by Mason during the second minute would resurface on 'Time'.

FREE FOUR
(Waters)

Another guitar-starred rocker, taking its title from the ostentatiously enunciated count-in "One, two, 'free, four!" and released as a single in several territories, but not the UK.

The lyrics are Waters' first direct reference to the wartime death of his father, a theme which would be of key importance to *The Wall* and *The Final Cut* and, in a more general sense, 'Us And Them' on *Dark Side...* Waters also manages to include a sideswipe at the rock'n'roll circus, bemoaning the need for yet *another* American tour. The latter lyrics were new for the album version, in the film there is a verse very reminiscent of the lines about "taking a slice" in 'Money'. There are other, minor lyrical differences elsewhere in the song.

STAY
(Wright/Waters)

Sung by Richard Wright, this appears to be a heart-melting love song, a genre not typically associated with Pink Floyd. However, there is a sting in the tail, when in the light of a new morning, the narrator cannot remember the name of the woman he wakes up with (a groupie, perhaps?) and wants her to leave.

ABSOLUTELY CURTAINS
(Waters/Gilmour/Wright/Mason)
Perhaps taking advantage of the new studio's facilities, Wright took the opportunity to play not only his usual Mellotron and organ, but something that sounds suspiciously like a harpsichord. The closing two minutes are taken up by the singing of the film's New Guinea natives – Pink Floyd were even ahead of their time with so-called "World Music".

LIVE AT POMPEII

Premièred: September 1972
DVD: Universal DVD 820 131 0 -11; 21 October 2003

Tracks: Instrumental; Echoes Part I; Careful With That Axe, Eugene; A Saucerful Of Secrets; Us And Them; One Of These Days I'm Going To Cut You Into Little Pieces; Set The Controls For The Heart Of The Sun; Brain Damage; Mademoiselle Nobs; Echoes Part II

Another important milestone in the history of Pink Floyd is this film, an audience-free performance shot in the amphitheatre of the Roman town of Pompeii, recorded in October 1971. Despite obvious recourse to studio reworking, the film, directed by Adrian Maben, captures the spirit of the era's live performances superbly. Also included are interviews and scenes of the band pretending to work on *Dark Side...* (when it was, in fact, already finished) in Abbey Road Studios. This includes the memorable David Gilmour quote, after being chided by Roger

Waters for allowing an impurity in his guitar sound: "Christ, where would rock'n'roll be without feedback" and the somewhat less significant Nick Mason utterances about his preference for apple pie *without* the crust.

There are two different versions of the opening instrumental, one used in the original film, the other on all the available video versions. Both are insignificant electronic doodles.

'Mademoiselle Nobs', recorded in a studio in Paris, was a version of 'Seamus', from *Meddle*, renamed for "Nobs", the female Russian Wolfhound who took lead, er, vocals, with Gilmour playing harmonica instead of singing, and Waters switching to one of Gilmour's Stratocaster guitars.

Most home-video releases of the film omitted the interviews and Abbey Road footage. It was available on Laser Disc for a time, and finally made it onto DVD in 2003. There was some surprise that the DVD featured a new "Director's Cut", with extensive contemporary interviews (Gilmour's accent sounds considerably less upper-class than in the 21st century), more scenes of the band eating, and new footage, whose soundtrack was heard over some of the original music – a bit like drawing a moustache on a Van Gogh. Thankfully the live material could be played, as the "Original Concert Film", but the "classic" film (with live footage and Abbey Road material, and none of Maben's later additions), was not included, to the annoyance of many fans. (It's worth noting that control over the use of the film in this way does not rest with the band.) Extras included a 24-minute filmed interview with Maben, which managed to be both interesting and informative, a photo gallery, a history of Pompeii, lyrics, album graphics (i.e. some pointless, low-quality shots of album sleeves) and "odds and sods" (more still artwork, with no explanatory text).

DARK SIDE OF THE MOON

Released 24 March 1973
as Harvest SHVL 804
UK Chart: #2, recharted 1993 (#4),
1994 (#38), 2003 (#17); US Chart: #1
First CD: EMI 7 46001 2; 1984
Remaster: EMI 8 29752 2; 25 July 1994
SACD: EMI 582136 2; April 2003

Without a doubt, this is the BIG one. Statistically, it should be playing somewhere or other on the planet during every moment of every day, with a copy in one in five UK households.

The record's release was not the suite's début, however, as the very first performance, subtitled "A Piece For Assorted Lunatics", was in early 1972 and was abruptly halted by a power failure during 'Money'. The title *Dark Side Of The Moon* is a reference to the occult name for the subconscious. However, Medicine Head released an album of that name in late 1971, so the planned title was changed to "Eclipse". When the Medicine Head album flopped, the original title was revived by the Floyd, but even they weren't sure exactly what to call their new, self produced, album. Original copies prefixed the title as **The** *Dark Side...*, as did the front of the first CD issue. However, later copies, and both the spine and disc of the first and latest CDs, all omit the troublesome definite article.

Dark Side... was to be the first of a run of albums with all their lyrics by Roger Waters.

The importance of his narrative was highlighted by the fact that this was the first Floyd album to have lyrics printed on its sleeve (although the recent CD reissues of earlier albums have had lyrics added retrospectively). The idea of linking songs with themes of madness, ageing, work and death – worries that trouble every one of us – came about in a band meeting in Mason's kitchen.

Recording started on June 1, 1972 and continued through that year, the first sessions to take place on Abbey Road's new, 24-track equipment. The album's engineer was Alan Parsons, then paid £35 per week. After receiving an Emmy for his work on the record and going on the road as Pink Floyd's sound mixer, he built an entire career emulating Pink Floyd's sonic soundscapes on his own albums. In the past, this has elicited some sharp comment from David Gilmour, but the hatchet appears to be buried, as Gilmour contributed guitar to a track on Parsons' 2004 album *A Valid Path*.

Even at this stage in the band's career, tensions were running high between Waters and Gilmour, and record producer Chris Thomas – who was managed by the same company as Pink Floyd, Steve O'Rourke's EMKA Productions – was brought in to arbitrate between them during the final mixing. This was done in such a way that all the tracks, with the exception of the break between the original vinyl sides, before 'Money', segue into each other. The making of the album was later discussed by all four band members in the 2003 documentary *Classic Albums: Pink Floyd - The Making of The Dark Side of the Moon*.

The impromptu spoken parts were obtained by Waters, who showed flash-cards to various crew members and studio staff. These had questions such as "when did you last thump somebody" or "what do you think of death" on them. The subjects' replies were recorded and extracts edited into the mix. One of the participants was Paul McCartney, although his contribution was considered too cautious to be used.

A quad version (Harvest Q4SHVL 804), had some subtly different mixes (notably the spoken parts on the final two tracks, as heard on *Works*), but these were closer to the regular stereo version than other quadraphonic and mono versions in the Floyd catalogue. However, the quad mix was reissued in Australia on pink vinyl, in 1988. A quad master tape, intended for vinyl pressings, was inadvertently used in the US for the first batch of CDs.

Despite only reaching No. 2 in the UK, and managing only one week at No. 1 in the US, the album's chart performance has never been equalled, and probably never will be. Even taking into account a couple of minor breaks, it was in the US top 200 for over 800 weeks – more than 15 years!

The album's saxophonist was Dick Parry, a relatively unknown session musician, but favoured for sharing the band's roots in Cambridge, where he played in groups with Gilmour. He was an inspired choice, and accompanied them on tour for the next two years, and again in 1994. For *Dark Side...*, he was, says Gilmour, asked to "play like the sax man in the cartoon band who did the theme music for Pearl and Dean's ad sequence at the cinema in those days".

Apart from Clare Torry's famous contribution (of which more below), backing vocals were performed by female session singers Liza Strike, Barry St. John and Leslie Duncan, plus veteran gospel performer Doris Troy. A pair of black women singers, Carlena Williams and Vanetta Fields, known as The Blackberries, joined the band for post-album performances of the suite. All in all, the band performed the suite at least 385 times until abandoning it for almost twenty years after the 1975 Knebworth festival. The BBC have a superb performance recorded at Wembley Arena (then the Empire Pool) in 1974, but although this gets an occasional airing, sadly the band have refused requests for it to be granted an official release.

Dark Side... returned in 1994 for many of the dates on the *Division Bell* tour, and is included whole on the live *P*U*L*S*E* album and DVD. Waters performed the suite on each of the 100-plus dates of his tellingly titled *The Dark Side Of The Moon Live* tour in 2006/7, and has thus performed it more times than any other band member. Nick

Mason joined him on several dates, and some were filmed.

The original sleeve is one of the best – and best known – in rock. A triumph of simplicity, it was designed by Hipgnosis and drawn by George Hardie. Hipgnosis offered the band several alternative designs. The meeting, according to Storm Thorgerson, "took about three seconds, in as much as the band cast their eyes over everything, looked at each other, said in unison 'That one' and left the room". The sleeve includes two deliberate mistakes: there is no purple in the spectrum, to simplify the design; and the rear sleeve showed the prism producing a converging spectrum – a physical impossibility, but necessary to allow opened out sleeves to be arranged end-to-end, forming a continuous design, or mandala, useful for in-store displays.

Vinyl copies came with two free stickers and two posters – one a collection of live shots, the other a night view of the pyramids at Giza. For some reason, both are different in American copies, while the Japanese edition came with a lavish booklet. The band had wanted everything to be presented in a box, but EMI vetoed this on the grounds of cost. Twenty years later, they relented and a limited edition boxed CD (EMI 7 81479 2) was released, using a digitally revamped master tape. The box also contained a new booklet, revised artwork and five "art-cards". A year later, the new master was used as one of EMI's series of reissues. Shortly afterwards, the album became the first Pink Floyd minidisc (EMI 8 29752 8).

For all its brighter sound and glossy artwork, the 1994 reissue's packaging is inferior to that of the original album and the first CD. Not only is the comforting familiarity of the airbrushed prism on the front lost to a harsher version taken from a photograph of a real glass prism, but the live and pyramid shots (the original posters were adapted for the first CD's booklet) have been replaced and the photogram backgrounds are just plain tacky.

In 2003, the album's 30th anniversary was marked by the release of a hybrid Super Audio SACD with a 5.1 channel DSD surround-sound version remixed from the original 16-track studio tapes by James Guthrie. It featured new Thorgerson artwork, the front cover being a photograph of a stained-glass design based on the original. SACDs use a higher sampling rate than regular CDs, and so have higher quality and more fidelity to the original recording. The SACD content requires a special player, so a regular CD version is also encoded, on the same disc. Fans were disappointed at Guthrie's somewhat conservative approach, feeling that he didn't make adequate use of the surround-sound capabilities, and angry that he ignored the alternate guitar and vocal takes used on the vinyl quadraphonic version. A spine-chilling surround-sound DVD version, reputedly from the master tapes of the original Alan Parsons quadraphonic mix, with a low frequency fifth track added (giving a 4.1 configuration, instead of the more common 5.1), was bootlegged in 2006, and could be downloaded on-line. Though the band rejected this mix in favour of Guthrie's, it's far superior, and the format can also be played on either DVD-audio or regular DVD equipment.

The album has been covered, wholesale, several times. In 2003, the entire album was performed, in reggae style, by a collection of acts on the Easy Star label, as *Dub Side Of The Moon* (Easy Star Records ES-1012, USA) with bonus tracks called 'Great Dub In The Sky' and 'Any Dub You Like'. In 2006, former Yes member Billy Sherwood devised and produced a version (Purple Pyramid CLP 1621-2, USA) with contributions by many notable artists, including Adrian Belew, Bill Bruford, Vinne Colaiuta, Geoff Downes, Larry Fast, Steve Howe, Robby Kreiger, voice actor Malcolm McDowell, Colin Moulding, Del Palmer, Steve Porcaro, Richard Wakeman, Edgar Winter, Dweezil Zappa and, notably, Pink Floyd collaborators Tony Levin and Scott(y) Page. As befits artists of such stature, they avoided making a slavish copy, and added their own interpretations and

embellishments, making it worth hearing, even for fans with numerous copies of the original. (Sherwood had earlier done the same thing with *The Wall*.) A similar level of invention went into The Section's *The String Quartet Tribute To Pink Floyd* (Vitamin Records CD-8469, USA, 2003), an unhelpfully named, instrumental version of *Dark Side...* performed by said configuration, without taking the lazy option of using electric instruments, which has marred so many other "classical" Pink Floyd covers. No less enjoyable was the delightfully quirky *Dark Side Of The Moon A Cappella* (Vocomotion Records VOMO 0105, USA, 2005), credited to "Voices On The Dark Side" and rendered entirely by mouth, right down to the sound effects and percussion. Dream Theatre, moe., Phish, The Squirrels, a host of "tribute" acts and, surprisingly, Voices On The Dark Side are among the bands who have covered the entire suite live.

SPEAK TO ME
(Mason)
Opening with a reassuring heartbeat, this introductory sound collage forms an overture to the rest of the suite, including sounds from the rest of the album, plus the manic laughter of road manager Peter Watts. (Trivia fans will be delighted to know that his daughter is the actress Naomi Watts.)

The piece's title was the catch-phrase of the band's then tour manager, Chris Adamson, whose audible contribution includes the famous "I've been mad for fucking years", which was much more prominent in live performances. Also heard is the "...even if you are not mad" spiel by Abbey Road Studios' doorman Jerry Driscoll.

Roger Waters has since claimed that he devised the track and that Mason's credit (his only solo credit outside *Ummagumma*) was merely a gift, though its working title was 'Nick's Section'.

Although listed separately on the 1994 remastered CD, 'Speak To Me' and 'Breathe'

are indexed as one track, as they were on the first CD issues. To confuse matters, the CD in the *Shine On* box set and the 30th anniversary version index them as two tracks.

BREATHE
(or BREATHE IN THE AIR)
(Waters/Gilmour/Wright)
More naming problems occur with this song, which is sometimes listed as 'Breathe In The Air' and sometimes as just 'Breathe', for example on the remastered and 30th anniversary CDs (the copy in the 'Shine On' box set managed to use both names). Perhaps the longer title is intended to distinguish it from another track called 'Breathe', on *The Body*, Waters' 1970 film soundtrack album recorded with Ron Geesin. They share their opening line and, with a little imagination, it is easy to hear how one may have mutated into the other. In contrast, the first line of the second verse is the title of a song which was originally a "hit" in 1939, when Flanagan and Allen sang it in The Crazy Gang's film *The Little Dog Laughed*.

A short section from a 1972 rehearsal is on the *Making of... DVD*.

Until using it on the 1994 tour, Pink Floyd only ever performed the track as part of complete *Dark Side...* shows, but Waters used it as a stand-alone song during some concerts on his 1987 tour. At Live 8, 'Breathe' and 'Breathe Reprise' were performed, for the first time in their history, as one song.

ON THE RUN
(Gilmour/Waters)
The title is Waters' representation of the stresses of being always on the go, whether as a touring musician or in any other career.

The piece was largely created on a VCS3 synthesiser. Waters is seen recreating the track at Abbey Road in *Live In Pompeii*, though by the time of filming the album was finished. Responsibility for the footsteps in the closing sequence was later claimed by engineer Alan Parsons. Roger the Hat, a Floyd roadie is heard saying "Live for today, gone tomorrow, that's me". An airport PA system (actually a studio recording from an earlier EMI comedy album) announces a flight to cities in Italy.

In pre-album concert performances, this part of the suite had been a completely different, guitar-based tune, 'The Travel Sequence', with a keyboard solo.

During concert performances, a large model aeroplane would descend on a wire over the audience, crashing onto the stage, to explode in a ball of flame, while film of aerial shots was projected behind the band.

For some dates on Pink Floyd's 1987 tour, the plane was replaced by a giant bed, echoing the *Momentary Lapse* artwork. New, Storm Thorgerson-directed concert footage was introduced, with a man strapped to a bed, being wheeled along hospital corridors at ever increasing speeds until it burst through a pair of doors onto a runway, and took off.

TIME

(Mason/Waters/Wright/Gilmour)

Perhaps most famous for its cacophony of chiming clocks, recorded as a quadraphonic demonstration tape for EMI by Parsons and still useful for testing and comparing hi-fi equipment, and suggested by him for use on this album. The lyrics address Roger Waters' concerns about ageing – remarkable for something written when he was just 28; and his fear that life was passing him by – ironic for someone about to score such a massive success. David Gilmour and Richard Wright, the latter backed by the session singers, take alternate verses, with Wright's having the more mellow style. Gilmour's guitar solo is unequalled, remaining one of his all-time classics. Early live versions were much slower, with some awful harmonies (the term is used loosely!) between Gilmour and Wright.

Waters' line about "hanging on in quiet desperation" is borrowed from *Walden*, the 1854 autobiographical work by American Henry David Thoreau, which reads "The mass of men lead lives of quiet desperation". After the song's final, pessimistic lyric, comes an extra verse, subtitled 'Breathe Reprise', which is missing from a bootlegged alternative take. The segment's working title was 'Home Again'. Gilmour performs a solo version, with acoustic guitar, on the *Making of...* DVD, which also includes part of Waters' original demo as an extra.

A US single release has Nick Mason's opening Rototoms reprised at the end, courtesy of a deft piece of studio editing. The song is used on *Echoes*, complete with 'Breathe (Reprise)'.

Live performances were accompanied by back-projected film of animated clocks, which was eventually released as an extra on both the *Making Of...* and *P*U*L*S*E* DVDs.

THE GREAT GIG IN THE SKY

(Wright; later Wright/Torry – see below for explanation)

This is surely the most seductive song about

death ever. At Alan Parsons' suggestion, Clare Torry was brought in to perform the almost painfully beautiful vocalese. She recorded several takes at different volumes and pitches and the track is a compilation of these. Although she improvised her part in the studio, Torry was for many years not given the co-composer's credit that many now feel she deserved, receiving instead double the standard flat fee – a staggering £30!

Torry obviously didn't hold a grudge, though, as she reprised her performance on stage, both for Roger Waters' New York and London shows in 1987, and with Pink Floyd at Knebworth in 1990. She later earned a much larger sum when the track became the first Floyd piece to be officially used for a television commercial, in this case for Neurofen painkillers. After seeking permission from Wright (who, as credited composer, then held sole authority to say yea or nay), the agency concerned recruited Torry to re-create the original with session musicians, earning her a repeat fee every time it was screened. In 2004, she finally

decided to take legal action to secure her due, and, in an ensuing agreement, which involved a gagging clause, was awarded a considerable sum of money, plus the right to be credited on future releases.

Early live versions, known as 'The Mortality Sequence', were fairly dire, comprising a speech by journalist and moral crusader Malcolm Muggeridge, a recital of The Lord's Prayer and taped Bible readings, from the Book of Ephesians, with a keyboard accompaniment. The track returned to Pink Floyd's live set early in 1988.

On *Dark Side* CDs, 'Great Gig' cross-fades into the following track, masking what was originally the break between vinyl sides. The track is used on *Echoes*.

The "I am not frightened of dying" line is Jerry Driscoll's.

MONEY
(Waters)
The album's other great piece of *musique concrète* is the speaker-hopping

rhythmic till-ringing which heralds its best-known song. This was created by carefully marking the original recording, cutting it into inch-long pieces and painstakingly reassembling it on the studio floor, so that the various tills and coins sounded right on the beat – a task which could have been accomplished in minutes had the band had access to a modern sampler and sequencer. The aggressive saxophone part was capably handled by Dick Parry. The spoken comments are all from Wings' guitarist Henry McCulloch, apart from "cruisin' for a bruisin'", which was spoken by Patricia Watts, second wife of Peter.

Roger Waters' reference to Lear Jets is ironic, considering that both Nick Mason and David Gilmour went on to qualify as pilots, the latter (who handled the song's vocals) at one time operating a company, Intrepid Aviation, to own, fly and promote his collection of classic aircraft.

'Money' was released as a single in the USA, using an edited version, a rarity only ever released in the UK on the vinyl-only compilation *Rock Legends* (Telstar STAR 2290). The single's chart success – it reached No. 13 – changed the band's fortunes forever. It also changed their audiences, and they were never again able to play quiet passages without being drowned out by noisy fans unimpressed by the band's more tranquil moments.

It is the most performed piece in the band's history, used as the encore throughout the 1977 *Animals* tour, played on both Gilmour and Waters' solo tours and at all Pink Floyd's subsequent dates. Gilmour has performed the track at over 780 concerts!

Waters produced a pseudo-live version for a single B-side in 1987 and Gilmour, when he appeared on Nicky Horne's Radio One show in July 1992, allowed the airing of a brief portion of Waters' original demo for the track, with the composer singing to his own crude, double-tracked acoustic guitar accompaniment. The demo is also heard on the *Making of…* DVD. Inevitably, perhaps, 'Money' is on the *…Great Dance Songs* and *Echoes* compilations.

US AND THEM
(Waters/Wright)

Richard Wright originally composed this tune as a simple piano piece for *Zabriskie Point*, with the descriptive working title of 'The Violent Sequence'. It was given just a handful of pre-*Dark Side…* live airings in early 1970, including a gig performed without their usual equipment, when it was stretched to 21 minutes long! Wright is seen working on his piano part in the studio segments of *Live At Pompeii*. It was released as a single in the USA.

The album version, unlike the original, is enhanced by Parry's saxophone, in a much more laid-back vein than his strident blowing on 'Money'. Waters sang early live versions, but Gilmour did the honours for the album, with Wright unusually providing the heavier singing on the angrier second and final verses. The anti-war, anti-hierarchy lyrics could have been lifted straight from *The Wall*, though roadie Roger the Hat's "short, sharp shock" may not have gone down so well there. The person who said he was "really drunk" was Wings' guitarist Henry McCulloch.

As well as being an occasional encore on the band's 1977 tour, 'Us And Them' was a regular in Pink Floyd's post-Waters concerts.

An early studio version has been bootlegged, with the sax solo mixed very differently and no echo on the vocals.

'Us And Them' is the fourth and final *Dark Side…* track on the *Echoes* compilation.

ANY COLOUR YOU LIKE
(Gilmour/Mason/Wright)

Believe it or not, this instrumental, a VCS3 synthesiser and guitar work-out, is the only track in the band's entire canon where the 'other three' wrote together, without Waters, while the latter was still in the band. The title is taken, indirectly, from

Henry Ford's oft-misquoted remark, of his Model T, that "any customer can have a car painted any colour that he wants so long as it is black", though the band knew it as something often said by Chris Adamson. Working titles included 'Scat' and 'Dave's Scat Section'.

BRAIN DAMAGE
(Waters)
This, the nearest thing to the album's title track (it is the only song to include the words "the dark side of the Moon"), and the following song, represent Roger Waters' only vocals on the album. They have always been performed as a pair, including the encores on the author's 1984 and '87 solo outings.

In *Live At Pompeii*, Waters is seen pretending to over-dub bass to a tape which already has his completed vocals. Later, Gilmour is seen supposedly adding further layers of guitar. A 1972 version is one of the few post-Sixties Pink Floyd out-takes to surface. Waters performs an acoustic version for the *Making Of...* DVD.

The lyric about "the lunatic on the grass" is taken from an unrecorded song Waters wrote during the *Meddle* sessions in 1971. Its title? 'The Dark Side Of The Moon'!

ECLIPSE
(Waters)
'Eclipse' demonstrates one of Waters' favourite writing techniques – when in doubt, write a list. This "list-o-mania" can be heard on most of his subsequent albums with Pink Floyd, as well as several of his solo works. The words were not written until, after a few live performances, the band realised that the suite needed some kind of ending.

The album closes with the heartbeat once more, behind which Jerry Driscoll cheerfully adds "There is no dark side of the moon – matter of fact, it's all dark".

Or does it? The pages of *The Amazing Pudding*, the independent Pink Floyd and

Roger Waters magazine, were consumed with debate for almost two years in the early Nineties, over a piece of music which could be heard *very* faintly during the final heartbeats. Some claimed it was a figment of readers' warped imaginations, but something resembling a string orchestra playing 'Ticket To Ride' could definitely be heard at the end of Driscoll's line, on the remastered CD, if the volume was set very loud. Other copies, such as the previous UK CD, did not seem to have the same phenomenon, but a whispering voice could be heard at 1'41". Explanations ranged from a Floydian joke to interference during mastering, and from the use of second hand tape to a performance in an adjacent studio being picked up. All seem equally unlikely.

WISH YOU WERE HERE

Released September 15 1975
as Harvest SHYL 814
UK Chart: #1; US Chart: #2
First CD Harvest CDP 7 46035 2
Remaster: EMI 8 29750 2

Following *Dark Side* was always going to be a problem for the band. Eventually, it took them two years, a great deal of heartache, an abortive experimental album, two (temporarily) abandoned song ideas, the appearance of a high-selling bootleg and the accidental spoiling of a master-tape before they were ready. It was worth the wait. The story does not begin in the studio, however, but with that bootleg.

In 1974 fans began to buy what they believed to be the new Pink Floyd album, *British Winter Tour '74*. This was, in fact, a well-packaged bootleg, with live recordings of three new songs, 'Raving And Drooling', 'Gotta Be Crazy' and 'Shine On You Crazy Diamond'. Although the latter would be recorded for this album, the other two (which were performed live, in vastly evolved versions, on the 1975 *Wish You Were Here* tour) were not committed to vinyl for another two years, after further changes.

The album was again produced by Pink Floyd, at Abbey Road studios. Although most of the music was composed collaboratively, all the lyrics were by Roger Waters. Tour vocalists Vanetta Fields and Carlena Williams, "The Blackberries", were among the guest musicians joining the band in the studio.

The recording sessions were very difficult for the band, who had to balance the pressures of success with the fact that they had now achieved all their ambitions. Mason was particularly distracted, since his marriage (like Waters') was breaking up and drumming came low on his priorities, but the rest of the band were equally affected by boredom,

exhaustion and a sense of malaise that made it difficult to concentrate on the minutiae of recording. Indeed, the band came close to breaking up at this point and Waters has said the album could just as easily have been called 'Wish *We* Were Here'. Nevertheless, Richard Wright and David Gilmour both now cite it as their favourite Floyd album.

The sleeve design, another triumph for Hipgnosis, has never been adequately transferred to CD. Initially, the album came in a black polythene wrapper with a sticker of George Hardie's shaking robot-hands over a background divided into four segments, depicting the four elements, Earth, Air, Fire and Water (this was the basis of the cover of the first UK CD). Inside the bag was a regular album sleeve with an inner bag. Each of the four faces depicted one of the elements, combined with someone who was "not there". The burning man (fire) is obviously absent, as he does not feel the heat. The character in the desert (earth) has no face and no arms inside his sleeves. The scarf billowing in the wind (air) concealed a barely visible naked female figure (a different version is used in the reissued CD's booklet), and the diver (water, again different on the new CD) makes no splash. The burning man was used on the front of CDs outside the UK, and the second UK CD release. Also missing from the CDs are the "frame breaks" – each of the four pictures originally spilled onto the surrounding area. Vinyl copies included a free postcard, depicting the splash-less diver. To complicate matters, even vinyl copies differ, with some territories using alternative photos of the burning man.

A quadraphonic version of the album (Harvest Q4SHVL 814) was released, although there are fewer differences between it and the stereo release than is the case with the *Atom Heart Mother* or *Dark Side...* quadraphonic remixes. The album has also been available as two different picture discs and on a variety of coloured vinyls.

SHINE ON YOU CRAZY DIAMOND (PART 1)
(Waters/Wright/Gilmour)

Premièred in France in June 1974, as one long piece, 'Shine On...' was one of three new tracks. The others, 'Raving And Drooling' and 'Gotta Be Crazy' were held over for *Animals*, where they would resurface with new titles. 'Shine On...', meanwhile, became the centrepiece of the album, divided into two suites to bookend the three conventional songs.

Initially inspired by Gilmour's melancholy guitar theme, the piece is also full of Wright's best ever keyboard work. Another of the track's high points is again Dick Parry's eloquent saxophone. The lyrics match the poignant sadness of the music and are unmistakeably about Syd Barrett – the only lyric in his *oeuvre* which Waters will admit refers directly to his former bandmate. During final mixing of the track, a balding, portly figure visited the band in the studio. No one recognised him for some time, thinking he was an EMI engineer, until eventually the penny dropped – it was Syd. As the band repeatedly played back the tape, trying to establish the best mix, he asked innocently "Why bother? You've heard it once already."

The recording of the track was fraught with more down-to-earth problems as well. The band decided that the first version was not good enough, so after several days' wasted work, began recording a second. When this was half done, they were dismayed to find that someone had inadvertently switched echo onto two of the tracks, rendering them useless, and work had to begin once again.

Confusingly, vinyl copies of the album subdivided this track into Parts 1-5, with writing credits and start times as follows: Part 1 (Wright/ Waters/ Gilmour); Part 2 (Gilmour/Waters/ Wright; 2'09"); Part 3 (Waters/ Gilmour/ Wright; 3'54"); Part 4 (Gilmour/ Wright/ Waters; 6'27") Part 5 (Waters; 8'42"). The vocals are, therefore, all in Part 5.

The drone at the start of 'Shine On...' is played on wine glasses full of water and is part of the abortive *Household Objects* album with which the band had originally intended to follow *Dark Side...*. Their plan was to record an album without the use of any musical instruments, and the band spent hours of studio time tuning strips of sticky tape and rubber bands – none of which would have been necessary had the Fairlight Synthesiser existed in 1975.

Different edited versions of the whole suite appeared on the *...Great Dance Songs* and *Echoes* compilations.

Both halves of 'Shine On...' remained in the set list until the end of the 1977 tour. Various permutations of the parts were performed throughout the 1987/9 tour and at Knebworth in 1990. They reappeared on the 1994 tour, and on subsequent Gilmour and Waters tours, and are included on *The Delicate Sound Of Thunder, P*U*L*S*E,* the *Live At Knebworth* DVD and solo releases, as we shall see.

WELCOME TO THE MACHINE
(Waters)

Roger Waters brought these verses to the studio, where writing was completed, making much use of his beloved VCS3 synthesiser. The track was then performed on the 1977 *Animals* tour, during Waters' solo shows and at most of Pink Floyd's post-Waters gigs.

The band usually refer to this as 'The Machine Song', suggesting that this may have been its working title.

HAVE A CIGAR
(Waters)

Since this was first performed live in April 1975, sung by Waters, it is not unreasonable to suppose it was written during one of the early studio sessions for the album. When Waters had trouble singing the tune, and Gilmour declined the chore in view of the "complaining" lyric (if only he'd known what was to come!), Waters suggested bringing in Roy Harper, a fellow Harvest artist and friend, for whose *HQ* album Gilmour had already provided guitar services. Waters later regretted the decision "not because he did it badly... it just isn't us any more". Even so, the song was deemed worthy of release as a single in mainland Europe, Japan and the USA, with different edited versions being used in various countries. Harper sang it but once again, joining Pink Floyd on stage at the 1975 Knebworth Festival.

In 1987 Waters again deferred vocal duties, this time to "Ace Mechanic" Paul Carrack, who guested throughout the *Radio KAOS* tour.

The line "Which one's Pink?" really was uttered by an ignorant US record company executive and became a weapon post-split, when Waters used it on one of his tour T-shirts.

WISH YOU WERE HERE
(Waters/Gilmour)

Unusually for the Floyd, the lyrics to this melancholy song, sung by David Gilmour, were written before the music, which came about after Roger Waters heard Gilmour killing time in the control room of studio number 3 at Abbey Road by strumming a tune he'd composed at home. The piece was not heard by a concert audience until sixteen months after the album's release.

The segue from the preceding track, made to sound like a cheap transistor radio, is responsible for apoplexy in more than one unsuspecting hi-fi buff. It was recreated live by the not inconsiderable feat of moving dozens of mixing desk sliders simultaneously.

Classical and jazz violinist Stephane Grapelli made an uncredited contribution, being paid £300 for playing just a few bars of the overture from Smetana's opera *The Bartered Bride*, which are barely audible during the closing wind noises. He was used for the simple expedient that he was handy, being in the process of recording in an adjacent studio at Abbey Road. The orchestral snippet on the radio was lifted from a recording of Tchaikovsky's *Symphony No. 4 in F Minor*.

Despite its belated début, the song soon became a live regular, featuring in post-split concerts by Gilmour, Waters and Pink Floyd. A notable rendition was at the band's Rock and Roll Hall of Fame induction ceremony, included as an extra on the *P*U*L*S*E* DVD.

Popular with band and fans alike, 'Wish...' appeared on both of the band's latter "hits" compilations and on band and solo live recordings, and was even Pink Floyd's last UK single, in 1995, as a live track from *P*U*L*S*E*.

SHINE ON YOU CRAZY DIAMOND (PART 2)
(Waters/Wright/Gilmour)

A continuation of Part 1, which opened the album. The piece was initially performed whole, but was split for the band's 1975

concerts, when 'Have A Cigar' made its début. Richard Wright plays the refrain from 'See Emily Play' in the fade-out.

On vinyl copies, this was subdivided into: Part 6 (Wright/Waters/Gilmour); Part 7 (Waters/Gilmour/Wright; 4'55"); Part 8 (Gilmour/Waters/Wright; 6'24"); Part 9 (Wright – his last ever solo composition for the band and his last of any kind until 1992; 9'03"). The vocals from Part 7 were added to performances on the later dates of the 1994 tour.

ANIMALS

Released: January 23 1977
as Harvest SHVL 815
UK Chart: #2; US Chart: #2
First CD Harvest CDP 7 46128 2
Remaster: EMI 8 29748 2

This album, which would turn London's Battersea Power Station into an unlikely tourist attraction, came about when Pink Floyd returned to the two songs discarded during the *Wish You Were Here* sessions. Assembling at their new North London Studio, Britannia Row, they reworked the songs, plus another Waters had written, about pigs. This gave him the idea for another grand concept, the album's Orwellian, anthropomorphic theme, likening human beings to species of animals. All that was then required was to re-title the songs, revise the lyrics to fit and add a short prelude and finale to bookend the album, not forgetting a few farmyard sounds to give

atmosphere. Because of the success of the *British Winter Tour '74* bootleg, this would be the last time that Pink Floyd would record material that had already been tested on the road.

To many people, the most famous thing about the album is its sleeve, for which Waters had the idea of photographing a flying pig (at least, an inflatable one) over the power station. Waters has, inexplicably, described the flying pig as a "symbol of hope". The sleeve required two days to photograph, on the second of which, the pig broke free from its moorings and floated off into the distance, generating many column inches of useful publicity. Of course, there is no reason to suggest that this was anything but an "accident".

Ironically, the resulting photo was not deemed suitable for the sleeve (although several shots are used in the reissue's booklet), so Hipgnosis reverted to their original idea of pasting a shot of the pig onto another of the power station. Waters gave himself credit for the sleeve design, much to the chagrin of Storm Thorgerson, resulting in a rift that kept Hipgnosis from designing sleeves for *The Wall* and *The Final Cut*. The dust jacket and CD booklet feature lyrics written out in Nick Mason's best handwriting.

The length of the three main tracks has prevented them from featuring in post-Waters Floyd concerts, although the tour that supported the album, dubbed "Pink Floyd – In The Flesh", where the album was performed in its entirety, was the biggest Pink Floyd ever performed with Waters in the band. They were augmented by a flying inflatable pig and rhythm guitarist Snowy White, who was also allowed to take the occasional solo. On the final date of the tour, Gilmour was so dissatisfied with the band's performance that he watched the encore, a one-off, twelve-minute blues led by White, from the mixing desk. Waters also hated the concert, but it did give him an idea, as we shall see...

PIGS ON THE WING 1
(Waters)

One of the most personal things ever recorded by Pink Floyd or its solo members, this is a simple love song for Waters' second wife, Carolyne Christie, and is therefore sung by Waters. Both it and its counterpart which closes the album sit in stark contrast to the heavyweight material between them. To further confuse matters, the third line was originally part of 'Raving And Drooling'.

The acoustic nature of the song made it unsuitable as a concert opener for the tour, so the album was performed out of sequence. It also featured in Waters' 84/85 tour, when it was accompanied by back-projected film of the pig over Battersea Power Station, but has not been performed since Waters split from Carolyne.

DOGS
(Waters/Gilmour)

A revised version of 'Gotta Be Crazy', a track which constantly evolved over the two years during which it was performed, even before being rewritten for this album. Waters' vitriolic attack on corporate climbers refers again to a metaphorical stone dragging down its victim, and his love of lists surfaces once more in the final verse.

The vocals are by Gilmour on the first four verses and by Waters on the remaining three. Unsurprisingly, given the writing credits, it is this track which is the album's showcase for Gilmour's guitar, which rises admirably to the occasion. Indeed, fans of his playing often cite this as the ultimate Pink Floyd number, although it was not recorded as easily as it could have been. The problems of self-producing the album in a new studio became apparent when an entire guitar part, of which Gilmour was justifiably very proud, was accidentally wiped by Waters and had to be re-done.

PIGS
(THREE DIFFERENT ONES)
(Waters)

Waters sees pigs as the people who think they know what's best for others, including Mary Whitehouse, the campaigner for TV censorship and religious bigot, referred to in the third verse.

All the vocals on this song are Waters' and all are electronically treated, but none so much as the Vocoder section after the second verse. Undaunted by what happened to his work on 'Dogs', Gilmour provides another climactic solo.

As one of the numbers written especially for the album, this was only ever performed by Pink Floyd on the 1977 tour, although Waters included a truncated version in a medley on his 1987 tour.

SHEEP
(Waters)

In 1974, 'Sheep' was known as 'Raving And Drooling', sometimes introduced with the unwieldy title of 'Raving And Drooling I Fell On His Neck With A Scream', which was, in fact, its opening line, a lyric whose last vestiges are now found in the penultimate verse. If we're led by dogs and pigs, Waters suggests, then most of us are sheep, blindly working our way towards an early grave, without questioning the systems which govern our existence. Such neo-Marxism is no doubt rooted in his socialist upbringing.

If 'Dogs' was Gilmour's guitar masterpiece, then 'Sheep' is held together by the bass part, although Gilmour claims to have performed this too. The cleverly written pastiche of the *23rd Psalm* ("The lord is my shepherd…") was originally performed by Nick Mason, although the version used on the album was recited by an uncredited member of the Floyd's support crew.

'Sheep' came close to being included in Pink Floyd's 1987 comeback tour, but Gilmour felt he couldn't sing Waters' vocal part with sufficient venom. It was, though, included on the ...*Great Dance Songs* and *Echoes* compilations.

PIGS ON THE WING 2
(Waters)
Effectively the second verse of the album's opener, Waters used this short song to ensure that the otherwise doom-laden record ended on a positive note.

When the album was issued in the USA as an 8-track cartridge, utilising a continuous tape loop, a bridge was needed so that Part 2 could be segued straight after Part 1. David Gilmour declined the job, offering it instead to Snowy White, who also joined the band as rhythm guitarist for the accompanying tour. This version is available on White's *Goldtop: Groups & Sessions* CD (RPM Records, RPM 154).

THE WALL

Released 30 November 1979
as Harvest SHDW 411
UK Chart: #3; US Chart: #1
First CD Harvest CDS 7 46036 8
Remaster: EMI/ Harvest 8 31243 2;
10 October 1994

On the final date of the tour which promoted *Animals*, Roger Waters was so enraged by the rowdy behaviour of a front-row fan that he beckoned him forward and spat in the unsuspecting fellow's face. Horrified by his own aggression, Waters began to put together a concept album about his feelings of isolation from his audience and the barriers which potentially exist between all of us. *The Wall* is the result. Waters started

Production credits were shared by Bob Ezrin, David Gilmour and Roger Waters, with James Guthrie listed as co-producer. Neither the sleeve nor labels of initial copies carried any mention of Richard Wright or Mason, an oversight which was speedily corrected for subsequent pressings. The album featured many uncredited session players with Ezrin and Gilmour covering for Wright, whose input was minimal to begin with and which lessened as time progressed. Near the end of recording, Waters gave the others an ultimatum: either Wright quit the band, or he would scrap the project, meaning none of them would recoup their Norton-Warburg losses. Wright reluctantly agreed, was only allowed to perform the live shows on a wage and was the only member of the band not present at the film's World Première at the Empire Leicester Square, London, on July 14, 1982.

Breaking with tradition, Hipgnosis was passed over in favour of political cartoonist Gerald Scarfe, designer of the animated back-projections for the 'Wish You Were Here' tour. He was commissioned not only to design the album sleeve, but also puppets for the stage show and animated films for promo video, concert and movie. Although the sleeve was devoid of lettering of any sort, a transparent, removable plastic label indicated the record's identity. Contrary to the claim of the generic sticker affixed to the 1994 reissue, its booklet does not include photographs, let alone "additional" ones, although the lyrics are printed in a larger, more readable size. A more notable quirk of the re-issue is that the tracks are indexed to begin and end in different places to the first CD. This is because rather than clean breaks between songs, there are frequently segues comprising pieces of *musique concrète* which could belong to either track.

The concerts remain the most spectacular ever staged by a rock band. As they played, a wall of cardboard bricks was built across the stage in front of them, meaning that they performed half of the show hidden from view. The wall doubled as a screen, onto which

work on the project in September 1977, just two months after the tour had ended. From the beginning, he planned it not merely as an album, but a theatrical concert and movie. The following July, he offered his bandmates a choice of two very crude demo recordings – one was *The Wall*, the other, which the rest of the band felt was too personal, eventually became Waters' first post-Floyd solo album, *The Pros And Cons Of Hitch Hiking*.

Recording began in April 1979, mostly taking place at Superbear Studios in France (used by Gilmour and Wright for their solo albums the previous year), CBS in New York and The Producers Workshop in LA. Some work was also done at Pink Floyd's (later Nick Mason's) studio at Britannia Row, London, but this was not declared, for company tax reasons, as the band were in dire straits financially, following the collapse of accountants Norton-Warburg, with whom they had invested vast sums of money.

were projected images, including Scarfe's animations. The trademark aeroplane, which crashed into the stage in a ball of flame, reappeared, as did the flying pig. The stage was also shared with forty-foot high puppets.

Owing to the complexity and cost of the stage show, *The Wall* was performed in only four cities: New York and Los Angeles in February 1980, London in August 1980, and Dortmund in February 1981. Further London concerts followed in June 1981, to allow for filming. Although the resulting films have never been seen publicly (at least, not legally) the intention was to include scenes in the movie version, which was directed by Alan Parker to Roger Waters' screenplay. Production of the film was to become a headache as Waters, Scarfe and Parker clashed over their interpretation of the screenplay. Parker, as director, had the final say, although all three regard the film as something of a compromise.

The Wall examines the barriers that we all – and specifically the tale's hero, a rock star referred to as both "Pink" and "Mr. Floyd" – build around ourselves to deflect criticism and to avoid facing up to our own failures. It describes Pink's breakdown as he sits in a hotel room during an American tour, and the concert he performs that night. It is partly autobiographical, partly about Barrett's decline and partly fiction, with a few incidents drawn from rock'n'roll folklore. The traditional disclaimer, seen at the end of the film, that "Any similarity to actual persons... is coincidental" can therefore be taken with a pinch of salt.

Perhaps understandably, the story has been described as over-convoluted and disjointed. Right up until the last minute, tracks were being both rearranged to keep the story coherent, and cut, to keep the threatened triple album down to a cost-effective double. It is certainly easier to follow the film if you are already familiar with the album, although, conversely, some aspects of the story are clearer on screen. It helps to realise that most of the story is told or seen in flash-

back, except for the scenes in Pink's hotel room and the subsequent concert, which Pink thinks is a Fascist rally.

In 1990, Waters performed *The Wall* once more, in Berlin, with an all-star cast, to raise funds for the Memorial Fund for Disaster Relief. In the summer of 1994, he announced that he was adapting *The Wall* as a stage musical, for Broadway. He later said that it would include new material.

As with *Dark Side*, there have been some notable cover versions of the whole work. In 2001, Canadian alternative country band Luther Wright and the Wrongs covered the entire album on a single CD, *Rebuild The Wall* (Universal Canada 4400161102), in bluegrass style. In 2005, Billy Sherwood produced *Backs Against The Wall* (Purple Pyramid CLP 1535-2, USA), a double CD, song-by song rendition featuring a host of notable musicians, including Ian Anderson (who, though he sang 'The Thin Ice', lamentably missed the opportunity to sing "skating away on the thin ice of a new day"), Adrian Belew, Vinne Colaiuta, Geoff Downes, Aynsley Dunbar, Keith Emerson, Larry Fast, Tony Franklin, Steve Howe, Glenn Hughes, Robby Kreiger, Tony Levin (superb, as always), Steve Lukather, Malcolm McDowell, Ronnie Montorse, Del Palmer, Mike Porcaro, Steve Porcaro, Tommy Shaw, Chris Squire, Fee Waybil, John Wetton, Alan White, Dweezil Zappa and DJ Jim Ladd. It's blessed with the same interpretive approach as Sherwood's later *Dark Side...* cover. *More Bricks* (Vitamin Records CD 8992, USA, 2006), has 12 tracks from the album, performed by a string quartet, on one disc. The December 2009 and January 2010 editions of *Mojo* magazine included a disc each of an exclusive version, *The Wall Re-Built*, interpreted by a number of lesser-known, but capable, bands.

Since Waters originally conceived the stage show and film at the same time as the album, it would not be right to consider any one of them in isolation.

WHEN THE TIGERS BROKE FREE
(Waters)
The film opens with the first verse of a song not heard on the album or in the concerts. The second and third verses were used after 'Another Brick In The Wall, Part 1'.

Roger Waters, the only member of the band featured, wrote it for the album, describing the death of his father at the Anzio Beachhead, one of the killing grounds of the Allied campaign in Italy in early 1944, but it was omitted for being too personal to him.

It was also released (as Harvest HAR 5222, in a superb fold-out sleeve with film stills) as a teaser single for *The Final Cut* (see entry under that album also) when that album was still intended to be a collection of 'Wall' outtakes and soundtrack material. It reached #39 in the UK charts, having entered them on 7 August 1982.

The promo video, using a compilation of scenes from the movie, can be viewed on Pink Floyd's official website.

MC: ATMOS
(Waters)
The concerts opened with this spoken parody of a concert Master of Ceremonies (MC) setting the "atmosphere" by warning fans not to take pictures, set off fireworks or otherwise enjoy themselves. The role of MC was performed by Cynthia Fox and Jim Ladd (Los Angeles), Gary Yudman (New York and London; heard on *Is There Anybody Out There?*) and Wili Tomsik (Dortmund).

The skit, which differed from night to night, only obtained its published title when the live album was being compiled. The version released is heavily edited.

IN THE FLESH?
(Waters)
The studio album opens with the barely audible words "we came in", which hardly make sense until, during the dying moments some eighty minutes later, one hears "Isn't this where". The opening bars of music also mirror the final track, while the last sounds heard are a simulation of the Stuka dive-bomber which kills Pink's father – and which killed Roger Waters' father.

This overture takes its name from 1977's *Pink Floyd – In The Flesh* tour. Technically, the band have never performed the track live, as each concert opened with the four-man "surrogate band" playing, while the real Pink Floyd waited, the audience none-the-wiser, in the wings. In 1980, this band, who also padded out the Floyd sound for the rest of the concert, comprised: guitarist Snowy White, Willie Wilson (drummer in David Gilmour's various bands between 1963-67, and on Gilmour's first solo album), Andy Bown (bass) and Peter Woods (keyboards). In 1981, Andy Roberts replaced Snowy White; both are heard on the *Is There Anybody Out There?* live album. The surrogate band wore masks to make them look like the real Pink Floyd – it is these masks which are seen on the cover of *Is There Anybody Out There?*

On the studio recording, Freddie Mandell contributes Hammond organ. Bob Geldof sang the version that was recorded for the film. Waters performed the track live on all of his solo tours, though the version on his live album, which borrows its title, loses the question mark.

In the narrative, our hero, Pink, is a rock star performing a concert, and about to suffer a breakdown...

THE THIN ICE
(Waters)
The first flashback is to Pink's birth and childhood. The idea of "the thin ice of modern life" may, perhaps, have been subconsciously influenced by Jethro Tull's 'Skating Away On The Thin Ice Of A New Day' of 1974. David Gilmour takes the first verse, Roger Waters the second, both live and in the studio.

James Guthrie and Nick Mason both drum on the studio recording. The master tape of the helicopter, which was recorded especially for this album, was loaned to Kate Bush for use on 'Experiment IV', the only new track on her *The Whole Story* compilation album, as she couldn't find another recording with an equivalent ambience. 'Happiest Days...' is also on *Echoes*.

ANOTHER BRICK IN THE WALL, PART 2
(Waters)

Otherwise articulate critics have used their – mistaken – interpretation of these lyrics as a stick with which to beat Pink Floyd. They see a rich, well educated Waters saying that there is no point in educating the masses. In reality, of course, Waters is warning that cruel and vindictive teachers are liable to turn children away from the liberating education that is their birthright.

An obvious choice for a single, 'Another Brick...' was released (as Harvest HAR 5194) in time for Christmas, with a new, eight-second instrumental intro and truncated guitar solo, fading just before the "how can you have any pudding" dialogue. With a video directed by Gerald Scarfe (included as an extra on the DVD of *The Wall*), it had the distinction of being the last UK No. 1 of the Seventies, and the first of the Eighties. It also managed to get itself banned in South Africa, after being adopted as a protest song by schoolchildren in the townships. It made the UK charts again a year later, reaching No. 17, as part of 'Never Mind The Presents' (Epic EPC9070), a light-hearted Christmas medley of reworded cover versions – "Hey, Santa, leave the booze alone!" – by the Barron Knights (also on their 1993 *The Best Of The Barron Knights* CD, Pickwick PWKS 4160). Waters later collected a British Academy Award (BAFTA) for 'Another Brick...', as "best song from a film". As a result of the single and album's success, Pink Floyd were later inducted into America's National Association of Brick Distributors' Hall Of Fame.

ANOTHER BRICK IN THE WALL, PART 1
(Waters)

The first "brick" in Pink's wall is the loss of his father, an incident drawn from Roger Waters' own childhood. His pained lyrics are delivered over a bubbling bass riff, with just a few staccato guitar stabs from David Gilmour. The song's working title was "Reminiscing". For his 1987 concerts, Waters performed this and the following two songs as one piece. A brief snippet of the number was prefixed to Pink Floyd's 1994 performances of 'Part 2'.

THE HAPPIEST DAYS OF OUR LIVES
(Waters)

Does anybody believe the hoary old myth that school days are the happiest of our lives? Roger Waters obviously didn't, although he did revive the track for his solo tours.

In the film, Pink is caught red-handed writing poems in class. The teacher recites one, humiliating Pink in the process. It just happens to be the opening verse of 'Money'...

The tabloid press made much from their discovery that the schoolchildren who sang on the chorus had not been paid for their contribution – the deal being that their school would be given free time in Britannia Row for music lessons. Their taped voices were also used at the concerts.

Wall concert versions had longer solos and a drawn-out ending. Cyndi Lauper sang lead on the version at Waters' Berlin concert, and Thomas Dolby contributed a keyboard solo.

In January 2007, it returned once again to the UK charts, reaching number two, as 'Proper Education', credited to "Eric Prydz vs. Floyd", with an officially sanctioned sample of the original. 'Radio Edit', 'Club', 'Instrumental', 'Sebastian Ingrosso' and 'Sebastien Leger' mixes were also available, some featuring rather more Prydz than Floyd. An accompanying video showed school children breaking into people's homes… to fit energy-saving devices and turn off unused appliances.

Naturally, Pink Floyd's only No. 1 single is on both the *…Great Dance Songs* and *Echoes* compilations.

MOTHER
(Waters)
Pink remembers his overbearing mother…

Roger Waters, who performed the song on his *Radio KAOS* tour in 1987, has pointed out that it is not an attack on his own mother (a teacher and communist member of CND), but overbearing mothers, and the potential of all mothers to hold back their offspring, in general.

The track used several uncredited session musicians, including Bob Ezrin (but not Richard Wright) on keyboards, Jeff Porcaro (but not Mason) on drums and Lee Ritenour on guitar. A much sparser, mainly orchestral, version was recorded for the film, with some very minor changes to the lyrics, which changed again in concert, where the line "Mother do you think they'll like this song" always got a cheer. *Wall* concert versions were extended at both ends and in the solo.

Sinead O'Connor sang the female role in Berlin, but fluffed her lines.

GOODBYE BLUE SKY

(Waters)

Initially opening the second side of vinyl with the song of a Skylark, 'Goodbye Blue Sky' mixes acoustic guitar with menacing keyboards and a fine example of David Gilmour's pastoral singing, to provide a tranquil interlude after the opening bombast, and an opportunity to reflect on the mental scars carried by Pink at the end of the war. In the film, the track came after the second part of 'When The Tigers Broke Free', to accompany a superb animated sequence. The child's voice belongs to Waters' son with Carolyne, Harry, who was born in 1977 and grew up to play keyboards in his father's 2006/7 touring band.

EMPTY SPACES

(Waters)

This instrumental was replaced in live performances, and for the film, by 'What Shall We Do Now', which is basically the same tune. The album's notorious backward message occurs here. For the benefit of readers whose CD players only spin anti-clockwise, it says "Congratulations, you have just discovered the secret message. Send your answer to Old Pink, care of The Funny Farm, Chalfont". The first CD issue mistakenly indexed this track and 'Young Lust' as one item.

WHAT SHALL WE DO NOW

(Waters)

Observant readers will notice that this song – another of Roger Waters' lists – is not heard on the album. It was dropped at the last minute, as material was re-sequenced and cut to prevent the double album from becoming a triple, but too late to have the lyrics removed from the sleeve, which was already at the printers (they have been excised from all CD versions). It was, though, used at this point at the concerts and in the film, where it accompanied more of Gerald Scarfe's animation. Originally, it came later in the story. Its working title, on Waters' 1978 demo of *The Wall*, was "Backs to the Wall".

YOUNG LUST

(Waters/Gilmour)

Pink is torn between his lust for a groupie and his love for his estranged wife...

Roger Waters asked David Gilmour to repeat his vocal performance from 'The Nile Song' for this "pastiche of just any rock'n'roll band out on the road", a situation in which Pink discovers groupies. Cinematographic train-spotters should note an early appearance by Joanne Whalley, as the only one of the groupies to keep her vest on; and Gary Olsen as a roadie.

The 'phone call where Pink's wife's lover answers the 'phone and then hangs up was staged, but the telephone operator is real and was unaware of the situation - all her comments were made under the impression that the call was genuine. The tape was also played at the concerts. Bryan Adams handled vocal duties in Berlin.

The 1978 demo had different, more autobiographical, lyrics.

ONE OF MY TURNS

(Waters)

Pink, disgusted with his treatment of a groupie, and at the same time saddened by his wife's infidelity and the disintegration of their marriage, throws a wobbly, trashing his hotel room...

The uncredited rhythm guitar was by Lee Ritenour, because, as David Gilmour put it, he "couldn't think of a good part to play". The groupie's voice was originally to be provided by Roger Waters. Thankfully, Bob Ezrin found a woman, Trudy Young, willing to re-do the part. Ezrin also plays keyboards. The song was a surprising choice for the B-side of the 'Another Brick...' single.

The original CD indexed this as two tracks, breaking as the mood suddenly changes midway through, while a typographical error on the label of some copies names the track – truthfully enough – as 'One Of My Tunes'!

During the film, *The Dambusters* plays on Pink's television at this point. The destructive rage was apparently inspired by a Roy Harper tantrum, backstage at the Knebworth Festival in 1975.

DON'T LEAVE ME NOW
(Waters)
Pink, like many needy and selfish men, is unable to understand why his wife leaves him, even though he catalogues the many abysmal ways he has treated her...

The film mixes action footage with the sort of animation that would have given Sigmund Freud a field day.

ANOTHER BRICK IN THE WALL, PART 3
(Waters)
Pink, rejected, declares that he doesn't need anything people have to offer him...

Again the lyrics differ from those on the widely bootlegged demo recording.

Live performances, particularly during the second round of *Wall* concerts, included an extended instrumental ending. A more up-tempo rendition is heard in the film.

The cinema version has the 1950 film *King Solomon's Mines* playing in the background.

THE LAST FEW BRICKS
(Waters)
This bridging sequence, added for the live performances, to give the road crew time to complete the building of the wall, reprised themes from the first half of the show, with choral "oohs" and "aahs", but no lyrics. Its length varied from night to night, depending on how many bricks remained to be laid. Previously known as 'The Medley', it also obtained its published title when the live album was being compiled.

GOODBYE CRUEL WORLD
(Waters)
Pink's wall is complete: he has isolated himself, totally, from his friends and loved ones...

This ends the first half of the record and concert, and marked the insertion of the last brick in the physical wall which separated the band from audience.

The octave performed on the bass is a Roger Waters trademark, harking back to the outro of 'See Emily Play', but most memorably heard on 'Careful With That Axe, Eugene' and 'Sheep'.

HEY YOU
(Waters)
The fact that these lyrics appeared in the wrong place on the original album sleeve was another indication of the last minute re-sequencing which took place as Bob Ezrin strove to keep the album within four sides of vinyl, and make sense of the story.

The song, which had fretless bass played by David Gilmour, was cut completely from the film version, even though it had accompanied scenes of rioting and looting in the early rushes. Stills from these scenes can be seen in the long-out-of-print photo-book which accompanied the film, *Pink Floyd – The Wall* (Avon, 1982, ISBN 978-0-380-81521-0), and the scene is included as an extra on the DVD release of the film.

When The Wall was performed live, 'Hey You' was played at the end of the interval, with no warning - the house lights were still up and the band were hidden behind the wall.

Roger Waters performed 'Hey You' during his 1984/5 concerts and it was used as an encore during the 1994 Pink Floyd Tour. Paul Carrack sang it at Berlin. The original is on *Echoes*.

IS THERE ANYBODY OUT THERE?
(Waters)
Pink realises his predicament, but it's too late...

David Gilmour admitted defeat and brought in session musician Ron Di Blasi to play the Spanish guitar, which Gilmour could play with

a leather pick, but not with his fingers, as it should be done. He also says that Ezrin, who plays synthesisers, should have received a co-composition credit for his contribution. The "seagull" noises could have come straight from the middle of 'Echoes', while the dialogue was lifted from an episode of the US Western serial *Gunsmoke*, called *Fandango*. The subtle use of a string synthesiser is also noteworthy, as it portends things to come. In concert, Gilmour performed the piece on an Ovation acoustic guitar, and the song gave its name to the live album from the shows.

The guitar part was rerecorded, this time by Gilmour, for the film, and is matched to a scene where Pink shaves off his eyebrows, just as Syd Barrett had once done. In Berlin, James Galway played flute.

Roger Waters later reworked the track (adding even more bone-chilling screams) for use in a cinema commercial for The Samaritans, which ended with the comforting caption, "Yes".

NOBODY HOME
(Waters)
Pink, still in his hotel room, reflects on his situation...

The line about "elastic bands keeping my shoes on" is a direct reference to Syd Barrett's behaviour during his final weeks with Pink Floyd. Similarly, the "grand piano to prop up my mortal remains" was said to be a dig at Richard Wright, the song having been written in the studio during recording sessions, at which Wright was under-performing. Indeed, it is Ezrin who plays piano on the recording, although Wright did play some keyboards. The New York Orchestra's strings and brass were chosen over synthesised versions.

Performing the song live (which he also did on his *Pros And Cons* and *KAOS* tours), Roger Waters appeared in a gap in the wall, in a "hotel room" with a table, chair, standard lamp and television. He would

switch channels on the latter, which could clearly be heard over the P.A.

VERA
(Waters)
Pink, flashing back to the end of the war, feels betrayed by his father's failure to return, even though "forces' sweetheart" Vera Lynn had promised "We'll meet again, some sunny day"...

Lynn's 'The Little Boy That Santa Claus Forgot' is heard at the beginning of the film. The station scenes were filmed on the Keighley & Worth Valley Railway, in West Yorkshire.

The New York Orchestra are heard again.

BRING THE BOYS BACK HOME
(Waters)
Joe Porcaro (father of Jeff) plays snare, leading a band of 35 snare drummers. The New York Orchestra are joined by the choir of the New York Opera. Roger Waters is the only member of Pink Floyd on the track.

A longer version of this, completely re-recorded for the film, sung by the Pontarddulais Male Voice Choir, was used as the B-side of 'When The Tigers Broke Free'.

The scene in the film, with the passengers singing to young Pink, was conducted by David Gilmour.

COMFORTABLY NUMB
(Waters/Gilmour)
Pink's manager (a brilliant cameo in the film from Bob Hoskins, who speaks volumes with his two words of dialogue) arrives to escort Pink to the concert, but of course Pink is in no state to attend. Concerned only for the financial situation, the manager fetches a doctor who injects Pink with something to "keep him going"...

This relates to a real incident when Roger Waters was persuaded to play a gig, despite suffering the effects of being prescribed

(Hendring HEN 2 086), with, among others, Sam Brown on backing vocals and Michael Kamen on keyboards. Pink Floyd performed the number on their 1987-9 and 1994 tours and in 1987 Roger Waters received so many requests for it from fans that he promised to include it the next time he went on the road. He kept his word by performing the track at the *Guitar Legends* festival in Seville in September 1991 and on his subsequent tours. In Berlin, Van Morrison took Gilmour's vocal part.

The song charted again, in 2004, in the guise of a splendidly camp, Bee Gees style disco cover version by Scissor Sisters, which reached No. 10 in the UK. It caused much annoyance to Pink Floyd's more reactionary fans, but reportedly drew congratulations from both Waters and Gilmour. Surprisingly Scissor Sisters had originally thought it only worthy of use as a B-side.

The song's popularity made it an obvious choice for inclusion on *Echoes.*

strong drugs for what turned out to be hepatitis.

Waters' words, differing markedly from those on his original demo, were put to a tune which David Gilmour had written at the end of sessions for his eponymous 1978 solo album. Gilmour aired a short section of his original demo on Nicky Horne's radio show in July 1992. The released version is an amalgam of the two takes the band recorded: a tight version favoured by Gilmour and the looser cut preferred by Waters and Bob Ezrin. Gilmour rates this and 'Run Like Hell' as the best two tracks on the album and has described it as "one of the last pieces of truly good collaboration that we [he and Waters] managed".

A vehicle for Gilmour's most blistering guitar solo, 'Come On Big Bum' (as he has been known to refer to it) has since become a live favourite, being performed during his 1984 solo shows (one of only three Pink Floyd songs he used) with Mick Ralphs handling Waters' lines, and, on one notable occasion, Nick Mason guesting on drums. Ralphs also joined Gilmour on a striking version performed at a charity show at the Royal Albert Hall, London in February 1996, to raise funds for disaster relief, and available on the *Colombian Volcano Concert* video

THE SHOW MUST GO ON

(Waters)
Pink decides that he must perform for his fans...

Roger Waters had wanted this, the opener of side four on vinyl copies, to sound "like" The Beach Boys and, in typical Pink Floyd fashion (i.e. nothing but the best), booked The Beach Boys themselves to record the vocals. This plan backfired when they decided the themes of the album didn't fit their carefully nurtured (but completely false) wholesome image, and went off to do their own tour instead. The desired effect was achieved by recruiting Bruce Johnston (who replaced Brian Wilson in The Beach Boys in 1965), Joe Chemay (who has worked as a session singer with The Beach Boys), Stan Farber, Jim Haas and John Joyce. Other than Johnston, they all appeared at *The Wall* concerts, including Waters' Berlin bash. Chemay, Haas and Joyce also made a guest appearance at one of Waters' 1987 concerts. Toni Tennille also sings on the studio recording. Its title in the original demo recordings was 'Who's Sorry Now?'.

Live versions included the extra lyrics which, although on the original sleeve, had been cut from the album in yet another attempt to reduce the running time. However, the number was completely omitted from the film.

MC: ATMOS
(Waters)
In concert, Gary Yudman returned, reprising his MC role at the start of the evening, but in slow motion. Like the first go, this one is heavily edited.

IN THE FLESH
(Waters)
Pink arrives at the concert, but thinks he is a Fascist leader, addressing a rally...

This is the same point in the narrative which started the story, and the song reprises the album's opening number (note the disappearing question mark).

Hammond Organ was provided by Freddie Mandell, Bob Ezrin played synthesiser, James Guthrie operated a sequencer and the "surrogate" Beach Boy and Toni Tennille sang. Bob Geldof again sang, or rather shouted, lead for the film version, which has no guitar or drums.

Although clearly a work of fiction, the lyrics in this and the following two songs have often been appropriated by those sad individuals who would adopt such policies in real life, to the point where racist graffiti in Liverpool in 1987 was accompanied by the crossed-hammers logo used in the film. Even many of the (real) skinhead extras involved in the film did not accept that Geldof was acting. Nevertheless, Roger Waters performed the track with great relish during his solo tours.

RUN LIKE HELL
(Waters/Gilmour)
Pink Floyd's disco number.

On first hearing, the sparse bass and guitar intro and the fixed disco-ish, military-style 2/4 rhythm of this song make it seem over simple, but the pace is ideally suited to the menacing lyrics, as Roger Waters was surely aware.

At the original *Wall* concerts, where it provided a musical backdrop for the reappearance of the flying pig, Waters took great delight in sometimes introducing this as 'Run Like Fuck', dedicating it to "all the paranoids in the audience", or mocking them, with a different tirade each night. The version on *Is There Anybody Out There?* has an atonal improvisation, starting about 4'45" in, with Waters' vocalese, which sounds like it was lifted straight from an *Ummagumma*-era concert.

The film version is shortened, despite being a particular favourite of David Gilmour, who again wrote the music while working on his solo album in 1978. He performed it on his

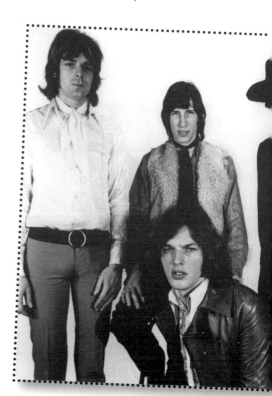

1984 solo tour and it is also on the *Colombia Volcano Concert* video. Pink Floyd performed it on their 1987-9 tour and at Knebworth '90, using a recording from Atlanta, November 1987 as the B-side of 'On The Turning Away'. Roger Waters responded by releasing a 'Potsdamer' mix of the track on the B-side of his live 'Another Brick In The Wall' single from Berlin. This was a truly awful dance version with tacked-on live applause.

Instrumental extracts were used in the *La Carrera Panamericana* soundtrack and the song was played again on Pink Floyd's 1994 tour, with Guy Pratt handling Waters' vocal parts. He would replace the "... send you back to mother in a cardboard box" lyric with "... send you back to New York...", or wherever the band happened to be playing. On the very last night of the tour, he sang "... send *me* back to Gala..." (Gala being Gala Wright, his wife, and daughter of Rick). Gilmour would sometimes include teasing riffs from other people's songs in the intro.

WAITING FOR THE WORMS
(Waters)
Pink uses a megaphone to describe the route of a right-wing march through ethnically diverse areas of London, into Hyde Park...

Note the strange laughter on the right-hand channel at about 2'24".

In Roger Waters' demo version of the album, where it was titled 'The Worms' – a symbol of moral and mental decay – it played a much greater part in the story.

STOP
(Waters)
Pink finally starts to question what he has become...

On the album Roger Waters sings, with Bob Ezrin's piano accompaniment. The rest of the band do not appear. Originally indexed to run for thirty-five seconds, the 1994 CD gives this track just thirty (thirty-one on the version

in the *Shine On* box set), making it the shortest piece recorded by the band.

In the film, the solitary verse is read by Pink, from a book of his poetry. He recites other "poems", some of which would resurface in 'Your Possible Pasts' on *The Final Cut*, and '5.11 AM (The Moment Of Clarity)' on Waters' *The Pros And Cons Of Hitch Hiking*.

THE TRIAL
(Waters/Ezrin)
Pink puts himself on trial, in order to save himself. He is his own prosecutor, judge and jury. The only possible punishment, and his salvation, is to tear down the wall, face up to his position and resume his interaction with society. The scream which accompanies the disintegration of the wall makes obvious the fact that this is not an easy thing for him to do...

The song, co-written with Bob Ezrin, who again provides piano in Richard Wright's absence, is hammed up by Roger Waters in the style of a Gilbert & Sullivan operetta. After the judge's comment that he is filled "with the urge to defecate", a voice shouts "Go on judge, sit on it!"

Tim Curry played the prosecutor at Berlin, with Thomas Dolby (teacher), Albert Finney (judge), Marianne Faithfull (mother) and Ute Lemper (wife) as the other participants.

OUTSIDE THE WALL
(Waters)
The album's coda, performed in lieu of an encore, is best explained in Roger Waters' own words: "That final song is saying 'Right, well, that was it, you've seen it now. That's the best we can do, really. And that wasn't actually us. This is us. That was us performing a piece of theatre about the things that it was about and we do like you really'."

The working title on the original demo was 'Bleeding Hearts', a name later appropriated by Waters for his post-Floyd touring band.

The album version has a children's choir and session musicians on mandolin and clarinet. The song was re-recorded for the film, again with the Pontarddulais Male Voice Choir and a brass section, and extended, to cover the closing credits.

Live performances included a variety of musical treats, differing from night to night, including David Gilmour on mandolin, Nick Mason on acoustic guitar, Waters on clarinet and Richard Wright on accordion. It was not performed in Berlin.

THE WALL (DVD)

Released in 1999 as Sony Music 501989
Special Edition: Sony Music 501986

The DVD of *The Wall* movie, described above, was remastered with Dolby 5.1 surround-sound. A later "Special Edition" came in a card sleeve, and included a reproduction of the film poster. Each included a raft of extras:

 ### THE OTHER SIDE OF THE WALL
A 25-minute "making of" documentary", filmed at the time of the making of the main feature, and rarely seen until this release.

 ### RETROSPECTIVE
A new, contemporary, documentary, featuring new interviews with Roger Waters, Alan Parker, Gerald Scarfe, James Guthrie and cinematographer Peter Biziou.

 ### COMMENTARY
Running commentary, recorded together by Roger Waters and Gerald Scarfe.

 ### OTHER
Other features included the missing 'Hey You' footage, the 'Another Brick... 2' promo film (both described above), photographic stills, and Gerald Scarfe's conceptual artwork, which had originally been used as a large-format book, to attract investment interest in the film, and which clearly shows Waters as Pink, with manager Steve O'Rourke and legendary tour promoter Harvey Goldsmith as roadies, ogling a topless groupie.

A COLLECTION OF GREAT DANCE SONGS

Released 23 November 1981 as Harvest SHVL 822
UK Chart: #37; US Chart: #31
First CD: EMI CDP 7 90732 2

Hastily compiled by David Gilmour as a contractual gap-filler and released with the Christmas market in mind, this greatest hits collection still interests fans by virtue of the inclusion of several alternative versions of the well-known songs it contains.

The cover was again provided by Storm Thorgerson and, like the title, is a play on Nick Mason's joke that their US record company probably thought of Pink Floyd as a dance band. In a similarly jocular vein,

Gilmour has said of the artwork, "It was so awful, I thought I'd get it cheap".

ONE OF THESE DAYS
(Gilmour/Mason/Wright/Waters)
The standard album version.

MONEY
(Waters)
The unavailability of the original version, due to contractual restrictions following a change in US record company after *Dark Side...*, meant that David Gilmour had to re-record the track. He acted as producer and played everything, other than saxophone, which was again provided by Dick Parry (lesser writers have claimed the work was all Gilmour's, overlooking the fact that he didn't learn to play sax for another two decades). James Guthrie co-produced and mixed. Even the original till ringing and rattling coin effects were used. An edited cut of the new version was scheduled for release as a single, to coincide with the album, to the point where a catalogue number (Harvest HAR 5217) was allocated and its B-side, 'Let There Be More Light', announced. The idea was abandoned at the last minute, but not

before some pink vinyl promo copies had escaped into the collectors' market.

SHEEP
(Waters)
The *Animals* version, probably selected as it is the shortest of the three key songs on that album, although Gilmour has said he had "quite a lot" to do with how it had evolved and was "quite proud" of it.

SHINE ON YOU CRAZY DIAMOND
(Gilmour/Waters/Wright)
This is a composite version, segueing Parts 1, 2, 3, 5, and 7 of the original, but with the last two minutes, the sax break, cut from Part 5. By editing together the two pieces from *Wish You Were Here* in this way, the piece was restored to something resembling the original version as first performed in 1974.

WISH YOU WERE HERE
(Gilmour/Waters)
The original album version, but with a slightly trimmed intro and outro.

ANOTHER BRICK
IN THE WALL PART 2
(Waters)

Uses the intro from the single version, but the album cut's ending.

pink
floyd
the
final
cut

THE FINAL CUT

Released 21 March 1983
as Harvest SHPF 1983
UK Chart: #1; US Chart: #6
First CD: Harvest CDP 7 446129 2
Remaster: EMI/ Harvest 8 31242 2;
released 10 October 1994
Extended remaster: EMI/ Harvest 5
76734 2; released 29 March 2004

The band's (or at least, Roger Waters') original intention had been that *The Final Cut* would be a soundtrack album to *The Wall* movie (one unimaginative working title was "Spare Bricks"), with the non-album and re-recorded tracks from the film plus some new material. Indeed, this was how it was first announced to the press. The film's credits also claim that a soundtrack album is "available".

By the time it was released, though, it had developed into a full blown concept album, fuelled by Waters' rows with film director Alan Parker, the Falklands conflict and its composer's despair at the state of Thatcherite Britain. For this was, in all but name, a Roger Waters solo album. David Gilmour openly admitted so, relinquishing his right to a producer's credit (but not the accompanying royalty share!), and went so

far as to say that there are only three good tracks on it. He was particularly unhappy at the inclusion of tracks which were rejected, on quality grounds, from *The Wall*.

Andy Bown, who had contributed to *The Wall* concerts, replaced Richard Wright on keyboards. Piano and harmonium were added by Michael Kamen, who earned a production credit for his work arranging the National Philharmonic Orchestra, the other producers being Waters and James Guthrie. Ubiquitous percussionist Ray Cooper also contributed. Among the eight studios used, all in England, were Hook End, then Gilmour's home, and The Billiard Room, at Waters' London residence.

The recording sessions became more and more fraught as time went on, Waters being determined not to compromise, as he no doubt felt he had during filming of *The Wall*, while Gilmour and Mason seemed to become, to him, mere session musicians.

Despite reaching the top of the UK charts (something neither *Dark Side...* nor *The Wall* achieved) the album failed to sell on the scale of its predecessors, perhaps because the proposed live shows to support it never emerged. Although Waters has performed parts, the recent incarnation of Pink Floyd appear to have completely disowned it. It comes as no surprise that they have never performed any of it in concert, but the decision, against Waters' strong protests, to exclude it from the *Shine On* box set is less understandable. The 1994 re-issue, mastered by Doug Sax, suffers the same adjustments to track-lengths as *The Wall*, but the only extra photograph is the one on the CD label. The 2004 reissue was remastered afresh, by James Guthrie, and has an extra track and a redesigned booklet.

The album's special effects utilised Holophonic sound, a recording technique which accurately captures three-dimensional movement. For best results, listeners should wear headphones, and close their eyes. It really does work, honest.

The album sleeve, depicting a World War II veteran's jacket in close up, with medal ribbons (top: the Distinguished Flying Cross, "for acts of courage, valour or devotion to duty while flying"; bottom, left-to-right: 1939/45 Star, for at least six months' non-operational service between 1939 and 1945, an Africa Star, for service in the North African campaign, and the Defence Medal, for three years' service) and part of a poppy, was designed by Waters and photographed by his then-wife, Carolyne's, brother, Willie Christie. The album's subtitle, "A Requiem For The Post War Dream By Roger Waters, Performed By Pink Floyd", underlined his almost total control over the project. Even so, the irony of such a strongly anti-war album being put out by a label belonging to Thorn EMI, then one of the world's largest arms manufacturers, seems to have been lost on him.

The 'solo' nature of the work was emphasised by the subsequent "Video E.P.",

in which Waters is the only member of the band seen – albeit hidden by shadow. The four-track EP (Video Music Collection PM 0010) was directed, to a screenplay by Waters, by Christie. Interestingly, the EP comprised the album's lead single and the three tracks thought by Gilmour to be up to scratch. It was later made available, free, on Pink Floyd's official website.

THE POST WAR DREAM
(Waters)
The album opens with its central character ("The Hero") listening to the news on his car radio, including an announcement that the replacement for *The Atlantic Conveyer*, a container ship lost in the Falklands campaign with 24 men, will be built in Japan, not in a British yard as had been hoped. (This scene is used at the start of the Video EP, although the track itself is not.)

Having said that, the first verse is very much in the first person, Roger Waters again referring to the death of his own father. His unfortunate use of the colloquial name for the Japanese, 'Nips', and the suggestions that "all their kids [commit] suicide" attracted criticisms of racism.

The references to 'Maggie' are, of course, aimed at Margaret Thatcher, the long-running Tory Prime Minister, architect of the Falklands campaign and more often the target of left-leaning singer-songwriters like Billy Bragg and punks like Crass than a millionaire rock star.

Michael Kamen's brass-heavy orchestrations add weight to the track.

YOUR POSSIBLE PASTS
(Waters)
The clanking of railway wagons, intended to suggest the cattle trucks (also referred to in the lyrics) which took Jews, Gypsies, homosexuals, disabled people and dissidents to German concentration camps before and during the war, are recorded Holophonically.

PINK FLOYD
THE MUSIC AND THE MYSTERY

1943

September 9
Roger Waters born in
Great Bookham, Surrey.

1946

January 6
Roger (Syd) Barrett
born in Cambridge.

March 6
David Gilmour born
in Cambridge.

1944

January 27
Nick Mason born in Birmingham.

1945

July 28
Rick Wright born in London.

1965

January
Billed as The Tea Set, a group comprising Barrett, Waters, Mason, Wright and Bob Klose make their debut appearance at Uxbridge.

1967

Late January
Pink Floyd record their first single, 'Arnold Layne', at EMI's Abbey Road Studios, which will be released in March.

April 29
Floyd play the 14-Hour Technicolour Dream at London's Alexandra Palace, alongside 30 other groups.

1967

June
Pink Floyd's second single, 'See Emily Play', reaches number six on the charts.

August 4
Floyd's debut album, *The Piper At The Gates Of Dawn*, released.

November 4
Pink Floyd open their first US tour in San Francisco.

1968

January 20
Syd Barrett makes his last appearance with the Floyd at a show in Hastings. Thereafter the group settle into life as a quartet with Waters, Wright, Mason and newcomer Gilmour.

1967

December
David Gilmour joins the group on guitar, briefly making it a five-piece.

1968

June 29
Pink Floyd headline the first ever free concert in London's Hyde Park. Also on the bill are Tyrannosaurus Rex, Roy Harper and Jethro Tull.

November 7
Ummagumma released.

March 23
Dark Side Of The Moon released while the group are in the midst of a lengthy North American tour. It will become one of the world's best-selling albums.

1970

January 2
Syd Barrett's first solo album, *The Madcap Laughs*, is released.

June 27
Pink Floyd perform in front of an audience of 150,000 at the Bath Festival, a three-day event headlined by Led Zeppelin.

1975

June
Sessions commence at Abbey Road for *Wish You Were Here*. Syd Barrett, by now living quietly back in Cambridge, makes an unexpected appearance.

1979

December 1
'Another Brick In The Wall, Part 2' becomes Pink Floyd's first and only number one hit single in the UK. It remains at the top of the charts through Christmas and into the new decade.

1981

June 13-17
A repeat performance of *The Wall* concerts are staged at Earls Court. This would be the last time the four-man Pink Floyd played together until 2005.

1975

September 12
Wish You Were Here released.

1981

March
Press reports indicate that Pink Floyd are suing financiers Norton Warburg for negligence. Apparently Norton Warburg has lost £2.5 million of the band's money on unsafe investments.

1990

July 21
Rogers Waters presents an all-star version of *The Wall,* outside at Potzdamer Platz in Berlin, featuring several guest artists in front of an audience of 250,000.

1984

May
Roger Waters' solo album·*The Pros And Cons Of Hitch-Hiking* released.

1984

March
David Gilmour's solo album *About Face* released.

2005

July 2
David Gilmour, Nick Mason and Rick Wright reunite with Roger Waters for an emotional four-song set for Live 8 in London's Hyde Park. Midway through the performance Waters says: "We're doing this for everyone who's not here, particularly, of course, for Syd."

1996

January 17
Pink Floyd are inducted into the Rock And Roll Hall of Fame at a ceremony in New York.

1994

October 12
The opening night of an unprecedented two-week run of concerts at Earls Court is halted prematurely when a section of seating collapses.

2006

January 6
Syd Barrett dies after a long illness.

2006

September
Roger Waters'
tour takes in
the USA.

2008

September 15
Rick Wright dies from can

2006

June-July
During Roger Waters' summer festival tour in
Europe Nick Mason plays drums at selected
dates. Most shows feature a complete
performance of *Dark Side Of The Moon*.

2009

November 11
Anglia Ruskin University of Cambridge and
Chelmsford award David Gilmour an Honorary
Doctorate for his outstanding contribution to
music as a writer, performer and innovator.

David Gilmour's heavy guitar solo is the only musical colour in Roger Waters' sparse landscape, and although this is a rewrite of one of the songs rejected for *The Wall* (Pink recited some of the lyrics in the movie), it is a perfect vehicle for the sombre subject. The lyrics printed on the sleeve and CD booklet include a couplet which is not sung.

ONE OF THE FEW
(Waters)

The character in this short bridge piece, and the next song, is the teacher from *The Wall* who, we now learn, is a war hero, returned to civilian society. The song's working title was 'Teach'. It is yet another example of Roger Waters' technique of using lists for song lyrics, taking its title from Winston Churchill's famous speech about RAF pilots after the Battle Of Britain: "Never, in the field of human conflict, was so much owed, by so many, to so few".

WHEN THE TIGERS BROKE FREE

(Waters) (Not on original version)
Though the 7" single's label had said "from the forthcoming album *The Final Cut*", this was not included on the original release, nor the first or second CD editions, but in 2004 it was inserted into the running order for a further CD reissue, having meanwhile had a CD release on the *Echoes* compilation. Each version has a different running length: 7": 2'55"; *Echoes*: 3'42"; *Final Cut*: 3'16". (For further details, see the entry under *The Wall*).

THE HERO'S RETURN
(Waters)

The "Hero", we also learn, is tormented by memories of the death of one of his air-crew, the gunner, and is unable to discuss this with his wife.

Despite being another reject from *The Wall* (it was called 'Teacher, Teacher' on the 1978 demo), this was used as the B-side to 'Not Now John', listed as "Parts I&II", the second part being an extra verse, not heard on the album. Sadly, the chance to add this extra material to the remastered CD was missed.

THE GUNNERS DREAM
(Waters)

The Gunner's – and indeed, the post-war – dream was of a world free of fear and tyranny, on a large or small scale, where the elderly can walk the streets in safety, where no one need fear secret police or terrorists (the latter evidenced by reference to the IRA's bloody 1981 attack on army bandsmen in Hyde Park). The penultimate verse is the voice of "The Hero". A superb sax break by Raf 'Baker Street' Ravenscroft is one of the album's musical highlights, no doubt helping to make this one of the three tracks acceptable to David Gilmour.

The lyric referring to "the corner of some foreign field" is borrowed from a World War I sonnet, *The Soldier*, by the poet Rupert Brooke, once a resident of the Grantchester area of Cambridge. The original lines read: "If I should die, think only this of me:/That there's some corner of a foreign field/That is forever England".

Pink Floyd's usual quality control slipped when this track was denied its rightful apostrophe on the album sleeve and labels, an error perpetuated on the CD issue.

The Video E.P. opens with this number, and we see that the hero/ teacher's son was lost in the Falklands. The Hero is played by Alex McAvoy, who played the teacher in *The Wall*, in case anyone has missed the point. Roger Waters' mouth and chin are seen, as is the back of his head, as he talks to a psychiatrist called "A. Parker-Marshall", a name derived from the director of *The Wall* movie, Alan Parker, and its producer, Alan Marshall. Waters used the song in his 1984/5 concerts.

PARANOID EYES
(Waters)
Simply, this is the story of the hero's middle age, hiding from his fears behind alcohol and a "stiff upper lip".

For the first half of the song, the music is almost entirely orchestral.

GET YOUR FILTHY HANDS OFF MY DESERT
(Waters)
The album's second side opened with the best use of Holophonic recording: a rocket is launched in front of the listener, passes overhead and explodes to the rear.

As if the earlier orchestration wasn't enough, Waters sings the opening verse, describing just a few topical acts of aggression, over a string ensemble – a far cry from the psychedelia of 1967!

Waters performed the short song on his solo tours – the version on his *In The Flesh* lasts under a minute.

THE FLETCHER MEMORIAL HOME
(Waters)
The title is a tilt of the hat to Roger Waters' father, Eric Fletcher Waters, to whom the album was dedicated. Waters proposes assembling a host of world leaders – at best inept and at worst corrupt and bloodthirsty – and applying to them the same "final solution" as used by the Nazis in the holocaust.

Another powerful guitar solo explains why this is one of the few tracks on the album liked by David Gilmour, and its use on *Echoes*.

Used to close the Video EP, its impact is lessened by the comic Napoleon, with his oversize snail. Thatcher and an Argentinian general are also seen arguing over possession of a croquet ball, with Winston Churchill watching on.

SOUTHAMPTON DOCK
(Waters)
Southampton was the embarkation point for a large number of the men sent to regain the Falkland Islands after the Argentinian invasion. It is also the place to which not quite so many men returned some time later.

The second verse again refers to Maggie Thatcher, as evidenced by Roger Waters lengthening a line in the second verse to "The slippery reins *of state*" when he performed the song on his solo tours.

THE FINAL CUT
(Waters)
In the movie industry, "the final cut" is the name given to the last edit of a film before the soundtrack is added. Waters uses the term to allude to both suicide and being stabbed in the back – as depicted by the jacket he wore in one of the small pictures on the album's sleeve. This showed him in military uniform, holding film cans, with a cleaver embedded between his shoulder blades – a comment on his relationship with *Wall* director Alan Parker. Around this time, he also had a jacket made with a knife in the back, which 'bled' theatrical blood as he squeezed a bulb in the pocket.

The lyrics refer to both *The Wall* and *Dark Side...* although the reference to the former is only discernible from the printed lyrics, being drowned out by a shotgun blast on the record. Gilmour again stamps his mark of approval in the form of a mellow guitar solo. Michael Kamen plays piano.

On the Video EP the track backs a montage of old, black and white newsreel footage of women at work and play through the ages.

NOT NOW JOHN
(Waters)
David Gilmour's only vocal on the album is in the guise of another character, someone who wants to bury his head in the sand and not worry about the state of the

world. The female backing vocalists are uncredited. The final verse repeats the same line, in broken Italian, pidgin Spanish, schoolboy French and finally Anglo-Saxon English, mimicking the stereotypical British lager lout on holiday in Europe.

'Not Now John' was the only single to be taken from *The Final Cut*, with the chorus suitably overdubbed "Stuff All That". For this reason, the altered recording is sometimes referred to as the "polite" or "obscured" version. Charting May 1, 1983, it reached No. 30.

The promo film for the single was the third track on the Video EP, with "typical" lazy British workmen apparently idling away their time, heedless of the threat of competition from Japan. If Roger Waters intended any other meaning, it was lost on most viewers.

Waters performed the song on his 1987 *Radio KAOS* tour.

 **TWO SUNS IN THE SUNSET**
(Waters)
As the narrator – be he the Hero, or Roger Waters himself – drives off into the sunset, in good old cowboy style, he is dazzled by a second sun in his rear-view mirror – a nuclear explosion. The children's voices probably belong to Waters' own son and daughter, Harry and India.

The drums were played by Andy Newmark, Nick Mason having had trouble finding the style Waters wanted. Whether he would have felt more inclined to persevere with the track if the atmosphere in the recording studio had been better is a matter for conjecture. Michael Kamen contributes piano, and the song ends on a sax solo by Raf Ravenscroft.

Unlike previous Pink Floyd concept albums – and, indeed, Waters' subsequent solo work – it is notable that *The Final Cut* closes in a very down mood indeed. The irony of the album's closing line, "we were all equal in the end" was not lost on those who followed the band's descent into a pit of writs, bitter press releases and catty remarks.

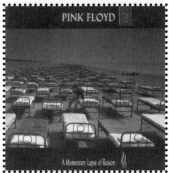

A MOMENTARY LAPSE OF REASON

Released: September 7 1987
as EMI CDP 7 48068 2
UK Chart: #3; US Chart: #3

In 1986, Roger Waters announced to the world that he had left Pink Floyd, which he described as "a spent force creatively", obviously assuming that the band would cease to exist without him. Pink Floyd's management issued a press release to the contrary, announcing their intention to continue regardless. These were the opening shots in the most acrimonious period in the band's history. While Waters busied himself first with abortive threats to block their plans through litigation, then with his solo career, Gilmour and Mason began work on the new Pink Floyd album.

It would take a book many times larger than this to detail all the arguments and counter arguments, but the gist of Waters' complaints (other than to say the band shouldn't continue without him, period) was that the album was an ersatz Pink Floyd, created by an army of "ghost writers" and session musicians. Although Gilmour denied this at the time, in a later interview he made the astonishing admission: "Nick played a few tom-toms on one track, but for the rest I had to get in other drummers. Rick played some tiny little parts. For a lot of it, I played the keyboards and pretended it was him." Even so, Nick Mason now had the distinction of being the only person to play on every Pink Floyd album, if not every Pink Floyd song.

Wright had rejoined his colleagues halfway through the recording sessions, but after taking legal advice decided not to join the band formally, but to remain on a wage. The credits pointedly listed his name in the smaller type used for the army of session musicians, and he is not pictured alongside Gilmour and Mason in the David Bailey portraits included in the album's artwork.

Lapse was co-produced by Bob Ezrin and David Gilmour, causing further irritation to Waters, since Ezrin, it was claimed, failed to honour a commitment to produce Waters' *Radio KAOS* in order to work on the Floyd project. Recording began on Gilmour's beautiful houseboat studio, the *Astoria*, then moved to a series of studios in Los Angeles, in order that the album could be completed by session musicians and the band could escape the constant stream of 'phone calls from lawyers preparing to fight Waters. Britannia Row was also used. Waters was replaced by one of the world's leading bass session players, Tony Levin. Pat Leonard, better known for his work with Madonna, contributed synthesiser and Jim Keltner and Carmine Appice both added drums.

Waters' departure also cleared the way for Storm Thorgerson to return to what many considered his rightful place as the Floyd's sleeve designer. His cover for this album is every bit as imaginative, bold and, indeed, expensive, as befits Pink Floyd. He took over

Saunton Sands in North Devon for two days, and arranged literally hundreds of hospital beds along the beach. Although it might have been easier to cheat and retouch his photographs, the line of beds really does snake along the sea-shore for two miles.

Asked what he thought of the album, Waters succinctly described it as "a pretty fair forgery".

SIGNS OF LIFE
(Gilmour/Ezrin)
Opening with the sound of a rowing boat, this simple guitar and synthesiser instrumental, built around one of Gilmour's 1978 demos, features Nick Mason's spoken voice and sets the tone for the rest of the album. It also came close to being the album's title track, until it was realised that it might be a gift to sarcastic reviewers. It was also used in the *La Carrera Panamericana* soundtrack.

LEARNING TO FLY
(Gilmour/Moore/Ezrin/Carin)
Based around a keyboard instrumental by Jon Carin, this tells the tale of David Gilmour's flying lessons. Already an accomplished pilot (and owner of an impressive fleet of historic aircraft), Gilmour would often absent himself from recording sessions in order to clock up flying hours and add extra, specialist skills to his licence. He allowed Nick Horne to broadcast ninety seconds of Carin's demo during their July 1992 Radio One interview.

Anthony Moore, latterly of Blackhill-managed band Slapp Happy, wrote the lyrics, assisted by Gilmour. To these were added a recording of Nick Mason running through a pre-takeoff checklist. An edited version of the song became the world's first CD-only single, (EMI CD EM 26), although EMI cheated slightly by making pink and black 7" vinyl copies available "for promotional purposes only".

Storm Thorgerson made the promo video, which features the 1987 touring band at their pre-tour rehearsals and an allegorical

film showing a native American turning into an eagle. His other film, featuring an aeroplane, was back-projected when the song was performed live. Both are on the *P*U*L*S*E* DVD as extras. The song is also on *Echoes*.

THE DOGS OF WAR
(Gilmour/Moore)
This title is derived from Antony's speech in Shakespeare's *Julius Caesar*, "Cry 'Havoc!' and let slip the dogs of war", via Frederick Forsyth, who used the term as the title of a novel about mercenaries, who are also the subject of this song. The lyrics, which bear no relation to the similarly titled track on *Animals*, were developed by Anthony Moore from an idea outlined by Gilmour, including the line "we all have a dark side", which Gilmour has conceded is a dig at Roger Waters.

One of the worst aspects of this fairly standard rocker is Scott Page's saxophone, truly a low point in Pink Floyd's history. Even so, it became a live regular, a version of which, recorded in Atlanta, Georgia in November 1987, was used to back some formats of the 'One Slip' single. A promo film for the track, directed by Lawrence Jordan, was shot at the same concert.

ONE SLIP
(Gilmour/Manzanera)
On this occasion, Gilmour's lyrics were put to music by his friend since his early days in Pink Floyd, former Roxy Music guitarist Phil Manzanera. One of the lyrics became the album's title, although this was very much a last-minute decision. Coincidentally (or perhaps not), Manzanera and Pink Floyd were both managed by Steve O'Rourke's EMKA Productions.

Another *La Carrera Panamericana* tune, 'One Slip' was the third and final single from the album (EMI EM 52) and was to see action on the 1987-89 tour, with just a few performances in 1994. In addition to the CD single, there were regular and pink vinyl 7" copies, and two 12" versions, one in a poster bag. All were backed by 'Terminal Frost', while the 12" and CD formats also had the live recording of 'The Dogs Of War' from Atlanta. In June 1988, it reached #50 in the UK singles chart.

ON THE TURNING AWAY
(Gilmour/Moore)
When this song opens like a traditional ballad, with David Gilmour singing almost a cappella, over a sparse keyboard drone, it is tempting to imagine him in an Aran sweater with his finger in his ear, performing an acoustic version to a bunch of bearded real ale drinkers in a back-room folk club. Sadly this is not to be, and clichéd, 'Wall'-like keyboards and unadventurous drums soon swell the song, before leading into a hearty rendition of Gilmour's rent-a-solo, which manages to save it from complete AOR tedium. The lyrics were again Anthony Moore's, with contributions from Gilmour.

When this was released as the second single from the album (EMI EM 34), it was backed by a live version of 'Run Like Hell'. As with 'One Slip', there were pink vinyl 7" and 12" poster bag singles, plus the usual plain 7", 12" and CD. Both the 12" and the CD versions had an additional, live, 'On The Turning Away', which, like 'Run Like Hell', was recorded in Atlanta. Charting in December 1987, it reached No. 55. The accompanying video, again directed by Lawrence Jordan, was filmed at the same concerts. A "bootleg" version is an extra on *P*U*L*S*E*.

In 1991, Gilmour performed the song as part of *Amnesty International's Big 30* concert.

YET ANOTHER MOVIE
(Gilmour/Leonard)
A lumbering song, lacking the dynamics which have given Pink Floyd the edge over so many of their imitators, it is again the guitar solo which provides the only excitement. Nevertheless, it was seen as one of the highlights of the album by Nick Mason, probably because of the attention

that was paid to the drum sound, with Jim Keltner and percussionist Steve Forman playing in a very large studio. Instrumental extracts were used in *La Carrera Panamericana*.

The film dialogue in the background is "borrowed" from one of Marlon Brando's monologues in *On The Waterfront* and from *Casablanca* (Bogart's "You've got to listen..." at 5'24", through to Ingrid Bergman's "What have I done?").

ROUND AND AROUND
(Gilmour)
An instrumental coda to 'Yet Another Movie', with which it was indexed as one track on CD. An unreleased five-minute version is known to exist.

A NEW MACHINE PART 1
(Gilmour)
Possibly the worst thing ever recorded by Pink Floyd, at least since 1970, with Gilmour's almost spoken lyrics pumped through a Vocoder and supported only by the weediest of keyboard tracks.

Gilmour has insisted that the title bears no relation to 'Welcome To The Machine'.

TERMINAL FROST
(Gilmour)
A mood piece, ripe with guitar frills from start to finish, overlaid with sax and keyboards and restrained vocalese, to which Gilmour at one time considered adding vocals.

The CD single 'Learning To Fly' included, as a teaser track, 'Terminal Frost (DYOL version)', where DYOL stood for "Do Your Own Lead", parts of the lead guitar track allegedly having been mixed out in order to allow budding Gilmours to play along on their own guitar/tennis racquet/hairbrush, although there seems to be no appreciable difference.

A NEW MACHINE PART 2
(Gilmour)
As the title implies, a continuation of 'Part 1'. Both 'A New Machine' and 'Terminal Frost' were written a couple of years before work started on the album.

SORROW
(Gilmour)
Thought by many to be about Waters, a supposition which Gilmour denied, claiming that his inspiration for the lyrics was a poem, although he says he cannot remember which. In fact, the opening lines paraphrase a line in John Steinbeck's *The Grapes of Wrath*. For the first time in his career, Gilmour wrote the words before the tune. His line "of promises broken" was another contender for the album title. This was another of the songs whose tune was used in *La Carrera Panamericana*. It also appears on *Echoes*.

The impressive guitar sound was achieved by the clever, if expensive, trick of having Gilmour play through a concert PA in the L.A. Sports Arena, then recording the result. Gilmour claims the guitar solo was recorded first take, with no subsequent attempt to better it being considered necessary. Short backwards passages can be heard at 4'44" and 4'52". No real drums were used, only a drum machine.

DELICATE SOUND OF THUNDER

Released: 22 November 1988
as EMI CDS 7914802
UK Chart: #11; US Chart: #11
Released on video on 5 June 1989
as PMI MVN 9911863

In September 1987, the new Pink Floyd began what was intended to be a short tour of American arenas. In the end, demand for tickets was so great that the tour eventually ran to 200 dates over a three-year period, also reaching Australia, New Zealand, Russia and Europe. For the tour, the three-man Floyd were augmented by Guy Pratt (bass), Jon Carin (keyboards), Gary Wallis (drums), Tim Renwick (a Cambridge veteran and long-time friend of David Gilmour's, guitar) and Scott Page (sax and occasional guitar). There were also a number of female backing vocalists, who came and went as the tour progressed. Initially, these were Margaret Taylor and Rachel Fury. When the Atlanta, Georgia concert of November 1987 was filmed for an abortive video and record (some tracks were used as single B-sides, and the show was scheduled, but never shown, by Irish television), three other vocalists, including Durga McBroom, were brought in, as she put it "to add colour". McBroom impressed sufficiently to be asked to remain in the band. (Taylor was replaced by Durga's sister, Lorelei, on the 1989 leg of the tour, which promoted this live album).

In August 1988, at New York's Nassau Coliseum, Pink Floyd recorded and filmed five shows for this two-CD set, produced by Gilmour, and a video, directed by Wayne Isham. The latter features additional footage shot at their historic gig outside the Palace of Versailles and was also available on laserdisc (Picture Music International PLMPB 000981) and, in July 1994, VideoCD (Picture Music International PMCD 4 91275 2; a now-superseded format, of lower quality than DVD, but better then VHS and still playable on home computers and most modern DVD players). There has been no DVD release.

The film is hampered by Isham's dreamy style – lots of slow-motion, soft focus, over-long cross-fades – distracting the viewer from the visual spectacle that is a Pink Floyd concert. They may suit a short promo video, but after a few minutes become incredibly wearing. The Isham-directed televised concert performed at Venice had the same problem, but much less so. Even worse is

the blue fog amidst which most of the concert seems to take place, giving no hint that the concerts were, in reality, very colourful affairs.

A possible reason for the abandonment of the Atlanta recordings arose when Gilmour admitted that, at the beginning of the tour, Wallis was playing all the drums and Carin the keyboards. Not until later did Gilmour consider that Nick Mason and Richard Wright had returned to being fully functioning musicians.

The sleeve was a Storm Thorgerson design, the light-bulb covered man representing the visual spectacle of a Floyd show, the birds' flapping wings the sound.

One of the tour's T-shirt slogans, "Pink Floyd – First In Space" seemed in retrospect to have been unexpectedly prophetic when, four days after the album's release, cosmonauts took a tape of *Delicate Sound...*, and a Walkman-style player, with them to the Mir space station. Gilmour and Mason attended the launch of the Salyut rocket at the Soviets Baikonur Cosmodrome, in Kazakhstan, previously the launch site for Sputnik and Uri Gagarin. They even recorded the blast-off for possible re-use on a future recording.

It is noticeable that every single track on the record, except the new material, includes Waters' name in the composers' credits.

 ### SHINE ON YOU CRAZY DIAMOND

To open all but the first few dates on the two hundred show tour, Pink Floyd chose 'Shine On... Parts 1-5'; a fine beginning, but unfortunately marred by a truly awful sax interjection, sadly typical of Scott Page's work on the tour. Video viewers are spared this, however, as only 'Part 1', David Gilmour's guitar introduction, is shown.

The rest of the first CD is taken up with material from *Momentary Lapse....*

SIGNS OF LIFE

(Video version only)
Although musically unspectacular, viewers do get the chance to see some of the special footage shot for the tour, although it would have been preferable if this had been spliced in directly, instead of filmed from the on-stage screen. This and other films feature Langley Iddens, David Gilmour's factotum on the *Astoria*.

LEARNING TO FLY

Apart from some ad-libbed guitar and inconsequential timpani during the last minute, this is little different from the album version. David Gilmour regularly allowed Tim Renwick to play most of the lead parts, opting to handle rhythm guitar while he sang.

Although the back-projected film is glimpsed from time to time, fans were disappointed that it was not included in full, feeling that its point was lost.

YET ANOTHER MOVIE

(Omitted from video version)
Despite some over-heavy echo on David Gilmour's vocals, this too is close to the album version, film dialogue and all.

The visual highlight of the track's concert presentation was Nick Mason and Gary Wallis' use of colour-shifting neon drumsticks, which were even more impressive from a distance, with the stage lights dimmed. Since the track is not on the video, Isham shifted them to footage of 'Time', but their original location is given away by the otherwise inexplicable cheer about half a minute into this track.

ROUND AND AROUND

(Omitted from video version)
Now indexed separately from 'Yet Another Movie', at thirty-four seconds this was once the shortest track released in the history of Pink Floyd, until the re-indexing of 'The Show Must Go On', on the remastered *Wall* CD, stole its thunder.

SORROW

Only marginally longer than the studio version, and not very different from it.

THE DOGS OF WAR

David Gilmour appears briefly in the Storm Thorgerson directed film, which was back-projected during the concert. Again, extra guitar livens the track up slightly.

ON THE TURNING AWAY

Differs from the *Momentary Lapse...* version only by virtue of a lengthened keyboard intro and an extended guitar coda in the film, but edited from the album.

ONE OF THESE DAYS

Disc two opens where the second, "oldies" set of the concert began, and is a greatest hits selection unblemished by *Momentary Lapse...* material. The second bass is a sample, played on Jon Carin's keyboards. The menace of 'One Of These Days' was the ideal time to fly Pink Floyd's new pig, which had added gonads, to avoid copyright problems over Roger Waters' pig, a sow. Even so, the video tetchily credits "Original Pig Concept by R. Waters". Although the pig is seen in the video, it never appears clearly enough to be properly appreciated.

TIME

Richard Wright's lead vocals are pleasingly confident, after so long out of the saddle.

The video shows some of the original animated film, by Ian Eames, to good effect, but the neon drumsticks are borrowed from 'Yet Another Movie', and don't belong here.

ON THE RUN

(Video version only)
New film, again featuring Langley Iddens, and emphasising the sense of paranoia, is seen behind the band (it's also an extra on the *P*U*L*S*E* DVD).

Not quite so clear is the bed which flew (down a wire) from the upper rear of the auditorium to crash in flames on the stage. At other concerts, this was replaced by a winged creature, nicknamed "Icarus" by fans, which flew away from the stage during 'Learning To Fly'.

THE GREAT GIG IN THE SKY
(Video version only)
Good though they are, the three vocalists who share duties here (in order: Rachael Fury, Durga McBroom and Margaret Taylor) can't match the power of Clare Torry's original. The out-of-place firework footage is from the end of the Versailles gig.

WISH YOU WERE HERE
David Gilmour and Tim Renwick duet on acoustic guitar.

US AND THEM
(Omitted from vinyl version)
Isham shows more of the back-projected film here than on other numbers, although it is galling to see some parts of it only in the corner of the screen. For once, Scott Page's sax adds to the song. Rick Wright's vocals are one of the few studio overdubs on the album.

MONEY
(Omitted from cassette and video versions)
Although this starts – Guy Pratt's odd interpretation of the opening bass riff and David Gilmour's oddly thuggish enunciation notwithstanding – as a straightforward rendition, it is extended to almost ten minutes, and ruined, by a series of solos taken by each of the musicians and vocalists in turn. Purists were offended by the fact that this "jam" changed very little from night to night on the tour, with Pratt's reggae riffing coming in for the strongest criticism. In fact, he has said it will haunt him to the grave. Serve him right.

ANOTHER BRICK
IN THE WALL PART II
(Omitted from video version)
Complete with taped school-kid vocalists, this too had a radically reworked ending, with guitar and bass solos. The peculiar fade was more impressive in concert, when the children's contribution was panned around the venue using the band's legendary "Azimuth Co-Ordinator" – a joystick which could be used to alter the quad mix, varying the signal sent to each set of speakers.

COMFORTABLY NUMB
Although bassist Guy Pratt often handled Waters' vocal part, the video shows Jon Carin and Richard Wright sharing it with him. Gilmour's acoustic guitar and some backing vocals were added in the studio, with an uncredited Sam Brown replacing Rachel Fury's part on the latter. There were also reports that the band spent an entire afternoon taping the track in an otherwise empty Coliseum, stopping and restarting some eight times until they got the take they wanted.

With anyone else, the idea of a mirrorball would be a laughable cliché, but in Pink Floyd's hands it became a concert highlight. This might have something to do with the fact that the one which rose during David Gilmour's extended guitar solo was absolutely huge and unfurled in mid-song, opening like a flower. Sadly Isham's film barely captures this, one of the most memorable – and talked about – highlights of the show. Worse, he edits the guitar solo (complete on the album) to the point of butchery. Also, due to bad editing during the first guitar break, Gilmour can clearly be seen to rest his hand while his playing still emanates from the speakers.

ONE SLIP
(Video version only)
Guy Pratt gets to show off his thumb-slap bass (whatever would Roger have said?) and Scott Page plays an electric guitar.

RUN LIKE HELL

Almost invariably performed as the last encore, with Guy Pratt again taking Roger Waters' vocal lines, this and 'One Slip' always seemed to be an anticlimax after 'Comfortably Numb', both visually and aurally, despite the arsenal of fireworks with which it was concluded. The intro is cut from the album, but is kept for the film.

KNEBWORTH – THE ALBUM

Released 6 August 1990
as Polydor 843 921-2
LIVE AT KNEBWORTH
DVD: Eagle Rock EREDV273

Pink Floyd played only one concert in 1990, at Knebworth Park on 30 June, alongside Robert Plant, Genesis, Eric Clapton, Paul McCartney and others. Pink Floyd's line-up included Candy Dulfer, replacing Scott Page on saxophone, the now familiar collection of backing musicians and backing vocalists: Sam Brown, her mother Vicki (who had appeared on stage with the Floyd at two shows in 1973), Durga McBroom and Clare Torry, who also reprised her vocal contribution on 'The Great Gig In The Sky'. Michael Kamen played keyboards on 'Comfortably Numb', adding, much to his colleagues' surprise, some completely unrehearsed improvisations. Perhaps that's why he's not mixed very prominently on the CD. Due to the stormy weather, the band's circular projection screen had to be dismantled before they took to the stage, but luckily after their specially made introductory film was shown. Fortunately, the suitably massive firework finale, which the band funded from their own pockets, was not affected.

The event was in aid of Nordoff-Robbins Music Therapy and the Brit School for Performing Arts and all the acts were Silver Clef Award winners.

The festival was broadcast on BBC Radio One and shown on TV around the world, except in the UK, where only highlights (if anything featuring Cliff Richard or Phil Collins' 'Sussudio' can be called a highlight) were screened. Selections were released as *Knebworth – The Album*, on three videos, and, later, on a two-DVD set as *Live At Knebworth*, with stereo, Dolby Digital 5.1 and DTS soundtracks. Pink Floyd contributed 'Comfortably Numb' to the album, 'Shine On You Crazy Diamond' to the video and 'Run Like Hell' to both. Sadly, the rest of the set, comprising 'Great Gig…', 'Money' 'Wish You Were Here' and 'Sorrow', has not been released.

LA CARRERA PANAMERICANA

Released: 13 April 1992 as: Picture Music International MVN 991 345 3
Reissue: Music Club Video MC 2134

Tracks: Run Like Hell; Pan Am Shuffle; Yet Another Movie; Sorrow; Signs Of Life; Country Theme; Mexico '78; Big Theme; Run Like Hell; One Slip; Small Theme; Pan Am Shuffle; Carrera Slow Blues.

In October 1991, David Gilmour and Nick Mason took part in a 2,500 mile motor race in Mexico, La Carrera Panamericana. They funded their involvement by accepting sponsorship and producing this documentary film, for which they provided an instrumental soundtrack.

The event recreated the original race, which was abandoned in 1954 after a spate of accidents. Gilmour and manager Steve O'Rourke drove one replica C-Type Jaguar, Mason and Valentine Lindsay (an employee of Ten Tenths, the company that manages Mason's extensive vehicle collection) drove another. Mason and Lindsay came eighth overall, but Gilmour and O'Rourke failed to finish after O'Rourke crashed their car, suffering a broken leg. Gilmour was lucky to escape with bruising.

The film, directed and produced by Ian McArthur, was premièred on BBC2 television in December that year, but the commercially released video is slightly different, with a few scenes replaced and some of the music used in different places.

As well as snippets of 'Run Like Hell' and tracks from *Momentary Lapse...*, several new tunes were used, produced by David Gilmour. 'Pan Am Shuffle' and 'Carrera Slow Blues' were the first Gilmour/Mason/Wright compositions since 'Any Colour You Like'. The remaining new pieces were written by Gilmour and all were performed by the trio with the assistance of Jon Carin, Guy Pratt, Gary Wallis and Tim Renwick. Despite initial suggestions to the contrary, the new material did not reappear on *The Division Bell*. There was no soundtrack album and as yet, no DVD release.

SHINE ON

Released 9 November 1992
as EMI 7 80557 2

A lavishly packaged box set including: *A Saucerful Of Secrets*; *Meddle*; *The Dark Side Of The Moon*; *Wish You Were Here*; *Animals*; *The Wall* and *A Momentary Lapse Of Reason*. All the albums were digitally remastered and came in a special set of black jewel cases which, when stood side-by-side, had the *Dark Side...* prism on their spines. Also in the box were postcards, a book and a "bonus disc", compiling both sides of each of the band's first five singles, again, all digitally remastered.

While this provided many newly converted CD buyers with an economical way to acquire seven of the Floyd's best-loved albums in one go, committed fans considered the band to have shot themselves in the foot. Although they could now obtain the early singles on CD, they had hoped for more rarities, in the form of unreleased tracks, outtakes and live recordings, instead of just albums they already had. What they got instead was a collection of rain-forest threatening packaging and a furry (as opposed to glossy) book whose myriad inaccuracies and omissions were overshadowed by the fact that the final page ended in mid-sentence. Perhaps the mysterious sounds at the end of *Dark Side...* had been added to drown out the cries of proof-readers being mercilessly flogged?

Unlike preceding CD versions, *The Dark Side Of The Moon* had 'Speak To Me' and 'Breathe' indexed as two tracks. On *The Wall*, the indexing errors on 'Young Lust' and 'One Of My Turns' were corrected. Of all the albums included, *Animals* probably showed the greatest improvement, losing the layer of audio murk which had marred the first CD issue. On the other hand, having only recently been digitally recorded, *Momentary Lapse...* needed no remastering.

In the jumbled up lettering on the CD labels can be discerned "the Big Bong Theory", once a contender for the box's title, but vetoed as "too drug inspired".

Although it has its own catalogue number (EMI 7 80572 2), *The Pink Floyd Early Singles*, as the digi-pack mounted disc was titled, was not officially available as a separate release, but has been bootlegged in a professionally packaged jewel-case.

THE DIVISION BELL

Released 30 March 1994
as EMI 8 28984 2
UK Chart: #1; US Chart: #1

Released on the same day that Pink Floyd opened their 1994 tour, the first thing most buyers noticed was that each format boasted a subtly different, but similar sleeve, showing two giant heads, designed and photographed by Storm Thorgerson with Ely Cathedral in the background. In each case, the heads were shot under different lighting conditions and were made from different materials. Further variants were found in the tour programme and song book, and on overseas editions.

Despite claims that the album had been written during jamming sessions involving the three remaining members of Pink Floyd, joined by Guy Pratt on bass, there were no writing credits for Mason or Pratt. Many of the lyrics were co-written by Gilmour and his girlfriend, later wife, former *Sunday Times* writer Polly Samson. Another helper was Nick Laird-Clowes, formerly leader of The Dream Academy, whose first and third albums Gilmour produced.

Although far from a Floydian concept album, *The Division Bell* has a general theme of communication gone wrong. The title is taken from the bell which is rung in the House Of Commons to warn MPs that a vote, or division, is about to take place. Author Douglas Adams named the album. He explained: "Dave Gilmour asked me to fiddle around with some of the album lyrics, which I did, though I don't think he used any of my suggestions in the end. The only suggestion of mine that I know was used was that the album should be called *The Division Bell*.

"I didn't think up the title, of course. I merely pointed out that the phrase was lying there in one of the song lyrics and would make a great title. Dave was a bit preoccupied about the title problem – they had to have the title by the following morning, and no one could decide what it should be. I said 'OK, I'll give you a title, but it'll cost you a £5,000 contribution to the Environmental Investigation Agency! Dave said 'Well, tell me what your title is and we'll see'. So I suggested *The Division Bell* and Dave said 'Hmmm, well, seems to work. Sort of fits the cover art as well. Yeah, OK'."

The album was jointly produced by Gilmour and Bob Ezrin. An army of session musicians was again called upon to contribute, including many from the previous tours: Jon Carin, Guy Pratt, Gary Wallis and Tim Renwick. Ezrin added keyboard and percussion and Michael Kamen was again responsible for orchestration. A surprising, and welcome, return to the fold was made by saxophonist Dick Parry. Durga McBroom, fresh from success with her own project Blue Pearl (to which both Gilmour and Wright contributed), returned on backing vocals, alongside another chart star, Sam Brown. More backing vocals were added by Carol Kenyon, Jackie Sheridan and Rebecca Leigh-White.

The CD case has Pink Floyd logo and the words "Pink Floyd" in Braille embossed along one edge.

 CLUSTER ONE
(Wright/Gilmour)
The album's instrumental introduction was also used in the lengthy intro tape which heralded the band's arrival on stage in concert. Bluesy guitar is predominant, over some echoey piano and drums that do not come in until near the end.

WHAT DO YOU WANT FROM ME

(Music: Gilmour/Wright. Lyrics: Gilmour/Samson)
Smothered with guitar straight from *Wish You Were Here*, and displaying excellent use of the backing vocalists, this apparent dig at Pink Floyd fans actually takes its title from something shouted during a row between David Gilmour and Polly Samson, though who said it to whom is not known!

A "bootleg" version is an extra on *P*U*L*S*E*.

POLES APART

(Music: Gilmour. Lyrics: Gilmour/Samson/Laird-Clowes)
Polly Samson has stated categorically that the first verse of this team effort is about Syd Barrett, the second about Roger Waters. Gilmour's vocal delivery harks back to his 1984 solo album *About Face* and is not a style he has previously employed with Pink Floyd. The Hammond organ riff during the middle-eight is blissful, but the point of the sequence preceding the third verse is unclear. Although this was performed live, it was never heard more than a handful of times, including one preserved for posterity as a "bootleg" on *P*U*L*S*E*.

MAROONED

(Gilmour/Wright)
A guitar-based instrumental, in places similar to the end of 'Comfortably Numb'. Pink Floyd's first and only live performance of the piece (there has also been one David Gilmour performance, at a charity event) occurred halfway through the European leg of the 1994 tour, in Norway, with back-projected film of whales at sea, as an eloquent dig at the host country's continued whaling activity. Luckily, this one-off was captured by a bootlegger, whose film is also on *P*U*L*S*E*.

Derived from a studio jam, its working title was 'The Whale Song', and Gilmour's guitar lick does seem to imitate whale song. In 1995, it earned Pink Floyd their only

Grammy Award, as "Best Rock Instrumental Performance".

A heavily abridged version is on *Echoes*.

A GREAT DAY FOR FREEDOM

(Music: Gilmour. Lyrics: Gilmour/Samson)
The title is a newspaper headline (clearly illustrated in the album's packaging), but its tale of the collapse of the Berlin Wall was covered much more effectively on Roy Harper's 'Berliners', on his *Once* album, to which David Gilmour contributed guitar in 1990.

The music is also weak, though whether this or the need for Gilmour to repeatedly deny that it alludes to the split with Waters (and his Berlin performance of 1990) explain its infrequent live outings is unknown.

WEARING THE INSIDE OUT

(Music: Wright. Lyrics: Moore)
Opening with laid-back sax from Dick Parry, Richard Wright's first attempt at writing music for the band unaided since *Wish You Were Here* still relied on outside talent for the lyrics, in the guise of *Momentary Lapse...* veteran Anthony Moore. Nevertheless, they could be describing Wright's post-*Wall* estrangement from the band in his own words. It was a surprise to hear Richard Wright record a vocal lead after so many years in the wilderness, but this treat was to be denied to live audiences as no performances are known to have been made.

David Gilmour handles vocals on a couple of the verses before closing with one of the album's more tasteful guitar solos. Two of the verses are sung by the backing singers simultaneously with Wright's vocals. The version on the vinyl LP was different from that on the CD.

The song was a regular feature on Gilmour's 2006 tour, on which Wright was a band member.

TAKE IT BACK
(Music: Gilmour/Ezrin. Lyrics: Gilmour/Samson/Laird-Clowes)
The music's resemblance to U2, especially The Edge's choppy guitar, attracted both comment and criticism, although, to be fair, The Edge's playing on U2's 'Silver And Gold' and 'Bullet The Blue Sky' owes a much greater debt to mid-Seventies Floyd.

When this was released as the first single from the album (EMI 8 81278 7), fans received another surprise: the B-side was a live recording, from the tour's opening show, of 'Astronomy Domine'. The video was directed by Marc Brickman, better known as Pink Floyd's lighting director, and is available as an extra on the *P*U*L*S*E* DVD.

 ### COMING BACK TO LIFE
(Gilmour)
The only song on the album where Gilmour managed to write all the lyrics unaided, a love song for Polly, opens with a bluesy guitar passage, followed by his breathy vocals. A simple rhythm develops as the second verse starts, but the guitar solo is restrained and the track never really goes anywhere. Gilmour performed this song, 'A Great Day For Freedom' and 'High Hopes' at his 2001/2 shows, as seen on the *David Gilmour in Concert* DVD.

 ### KEEP TALKING
(Music: Gilmour/Wright. Lyrics: Gilmour/Samson)
The opening monologue, more familiar as a British Telecom advert, is the words and voice of physicist Stephen Hawking, author of the famous and unfathomable *A Brief History Of Time*, who can communicate only via a speech-synthesising computer owing to motor-neurone disease.

Gilmour's use of Vocoder is very reminiscent of 'Pigs (Three Different Ones)', although some of his guitar is more typical of *The Wall* and *The Final Cut*.

To mark their record-breaking fourteen nights at London's Earls Court in October 1994,

a "radio edit" of the track appeared on a double A-side single with 'High Hopes'. The song is also on *Echoes*.

 ### LOST FOR WORDS
(Music: Gilmour. Lyrics: Gilmour/Samson)
Gilmour has denied that the lyrics – and particularly the final verse – refer to his former colleague, Roger Waters, despite fans' and critics' assumptions to the contrary. This may explain why it graced only a few 1994 concerts.

The opening footsteps, rattling chain and closing gate, plus the boxing announcement after the third verse, are among the last vestiges of the *musique concrète* which has been a trademark of the band's work for so many years.

 ### HIGH HOPES
(Music: Gilmour. Lyrics: Gilmour/Samson)
David Gilmour has admitted that this, the first thing he wrote for the project, is more personal than his usual style, and that it set

the tone for the rest of the album. Its middle-eight Spanish guitar and marching drums, with orchestral backing, sound like leftovers from 'The Wall'.

The bell which bookends the track is not the parliamentary Division Bell, but may be intended to represent one at a Cambridge College, or those of Ely Cathedral, both of which feature in Storm Thorgerson's promo video for the song, as does the Gilmour family's former home in Cambridge.

A "radio edit" of 'High Hopes' became the album's second single (EMI 8 81773 2) where, although presented as a double A-side with 'Keep Talking', it appeared to be the lead track: not only were its lyrics reproduced on the sleeve, but the front cover was from its promotional video, as were the images on the seven "film cards" included in a limited edition package. The cards were also included with a 12" coloured, etched vinyl edition. The extra track in all cases was a live version of 'One Of These Days'. It reached No. 26 in the UK singles chart. Possibly the last-ever Pink Floyd studio single, the song is also on *Echoes*.

The last thing heard on the album – it's very quiet – is a recording of Polly Samson's son Charlie hanging up the telephone on Floyd

manager Steve O'Rourke, emphasising the album's theme of poor communications. This is the band's witty response to O'Rourke's constant requests to be allowed to play a few notes on a Floyd album.

P*U*L*S*E

Released 30 May 1995
as a boxed CD, EMI 8 32700 2
UK Chart: #1, recharted 2006 (#34);
US Chart: #1
Regular CD version: EMI 4 91436 2

Tracks: Shine On You Crazy Diamond; Astronomy Domine; What Do You Want From Me; Learning To Fly; Keep Talking; Coming Back To Life; Hey You; Great Day For Freedom; Sorrow; High Hopes; Wish You

Were Here; Comfortably Numb; Run Like Hell; Speak To Me; Breathe (In The Air); On The Run; Time; Great Gig In The Sky; Money; Us And Them; Any Colour You Like; Brain Damage; Eclipse; Wish You Were Here; Comfortably Numb; Run Like Hell; on cassette and vinyl only: One Of These Days; on cassette only: Soundscape

To promote *The Division Bell*, the band embarked on another gigantic world tour, breaking records that have since been surpassed only by The Rolling Stones and U2.

Jon Carin, Guy Pratt, Gary Wallis, Tim Renwick, Durga McBroom and Sam Brown again joined David Gilmour, Nick Mason and Richard Wright (a full member of the band once again), plus a third vocalist, Claudia Fontaine, and for a tour of America and Europe. Fans were particularly glad to see Dick Parry back with the group.

A few dates on the tour had a set list which included, as the second half, the entire *Dark Side...* suite; its first performance by the band since 1975. Gilmour reportedly invited Roger Waters to perform at one of the London shows, but his agent replied that he was "busy".

This live album, pronounced and sometimes written as *"Pulse"*, was recorded at Earls Court, London from 13-21 October 1984, with some material earlier on the tour, and is thus not the same as the film version, described below. Gilmour and producer James Guthrie insist that no studio overdubs were made, unlike those for *The Delicate Sound Of Thunder*. However, some deficiencies were corrected by editing in solos and vocal lines from different performances.

The album (and the DVD's stereo soundtrack) uses QSound, a successor to Holophonics, which creates the impression of surround-sound on stereo systems, but without requiring the listener to use headphones.

Initial copies of the CD came in a strong cardboard slip-case, in which was embedded a red LED, set to pulse at the rate of an average human heart-beat, echoing the opening of *Dark Side....* There are even websites on which fans explain how to replace the AA battery which powers the LED, but no doubt most owners didn't bother, and the battery ended up in landfill – a strange idea, for an album recorded at concerts whose proceeds were donated to a number of charities, including Greenpeace.

See below for a track-by-track analysis.

P*U*L*S*E (Film version)

Released on video in 1995 as Picture Music International MVD 4 91436 3 DVD released 10 July 2006 as EMI 3 491436 9

Tracks: Shine On You Crazy Diamond (Concert Version); Learning To Fly; High Hopes; Take It Back; Coming Back To Life; Sorrow; Keep Talking; Another Brick In The Wall (Part 2); One Of These Days; Speak to Me; Breathe; On The Run; Time; The Great Gig In The Sky; Money; Us And Them; Any Colour You Like; Brain Damage; Eclipse; Wish You Were Here; Comfortably Numb; Run Like Hell

The *Division Bell* tour was filmed on October 20, 1994 at Earls Court, by director David Mallett, and released the next year as a 22-track home video. Over a decade later, after

many delays as extra features were compiled, a DVD was released. With over four hours of content, it was well worth waiting for, giving a much better impression of what it was like to be at Pink Floyd's post-Waters shows than does *Delicate Sound...*

As well as rectifying most of the faults of the *Delicate Sound Of Thunder* film, an entire 145-minute show, split over two discs, was featured, with QSound stereo, DTS and Dolby Digital 5.1 soundtracks, the latter offering a higher bit-rate option, giving better quality on more modern equipment.

Taking the contents of the various formats together:

SHINE ON YOU CRAZY DIAMOND

Titled as 'Shine On You Crazy Diamond (Concert Version)' on the DVD, this included Parts 1-5 and 7 of the original. The back-projected film, by Storm Thorgerson, was new for these concerts. The orange, plum and matches motif relates to an incident involving Syd Barrett, and is also seen on the *Syd Barrett* sleeve. Fans soon learned from on-line chat that if this opened the show, they would hear all of *Dark Side...* in the second half. If not, it would open the second set.

ASTRONOMY DOMINE

(Not on film)

Performed by just David Gilmour, Nick Mason, Richard Wright and Guy Pratt, with Gilmour and Wright sharing the vocals, this opened most dates on the tour, but, like other tracks on the album but not the DVD, was not played at shows where the complete *Dark Side...* was in the set list.

WHAT DO YOU WANT FROM ME

(Not on film)

The version on the album was recorded at the Studi di Cinecitta in Rome, on September 21, 1994. Richard Wright's keyboard introduction sounds like Seventies lounge music.

Although not included on the DVD's main programme, a "bootleg" version is included as an extra.

LEARNING TO FLY

Tim Renwick again took the solos.

The two pieces of back-projected film show an aircraft taking off, with a manic air traffic controller, and are the same as those used in 1987. They bear no relation to the promotional video for the 1987 single, which is included on this DVD as an extra.

KEEP TALKING

Recorded at the Niedersachsenstadion, Hannover, Germany on August 17, 1994 this is the earliest performance on the album.

TAKE IT BACK

(Not on album)

A workmanlike re-run of the album version, it's hard to see why this visually unremarkable performance was thought worthy of inclusion over other tracks, except perhaps to embarrass Guy Pratt by reminding the world of his strange "dancing".

COMING BACK TO LIFE

Generally, this was only performed on nights when *Dark Side...* was in the set list, and even then, not always. Again, it's a pedestrian run-through.

HEY YOU

(Not on film)

Spliced together from two Earls Court shows. David Gilmour shares lead vocals with Jon Carin, who takes the final verse. Despite its position on the album, this was used as one of the encores on non-*Dark Side...* nights.

GREAT DAY FOR FREEDOM

(Not on film)

Either this or 'On The Turning Away' was played, but rarely both, when *Dark Side...* wasn't in the set-list.

SORROW
Recorded in Rome on 20 September.

 ### HIGH HOPES
Compiled from two different nights at Earls Court, with Jon Carin again sharing the lead vocal.

Storm Thorgerson's back-projected film is very similar to the single's video, and includes scenes of Ely Cathedral, and places around Cambridge.

 ### ANOTHER BRICK IN THE WALL (PART 2)
Guy Pratt and Tim Renwick share the vocals with David Gilmour. The sound effects are lifted from 'The Happiest Days Of Our Lives'. Renwick takes a solo, very different to anything performed by Gilmour, but Guy Pratt's thumb-slap bass is worrying.

 ### ONE OF THESE DAYS
(Not on CD)
Oddly included on the cassette and vinyl release, and in the film, but not the CD, this version has an extended middle section, with a bass improvisation by Guy Pratt. In place of pigs, these shows had boars, with tusks, which, instead of flying, waved about rather ineffectively from each side of the stage while this track was played.

 ### SPEAK TO ME
The second half of the concert, and the second CD and DVD discs, started with a heartbeat...

Two different back-projections are included on the DVD; one from 1994 and the rather disturbing 1987 version.

 ### BREATHE
Called 'Breathe In The Air' on the DVD. Jon Carin shares lead vocals with David Gilmour.

 ### ON THE RUN
The DVD includes the full 1987 film footage, with Langley Iddens going on a nightmarish journey in his hospital bed.

 ### TIME
Compiled form four dates at three venues.

The DVD includes two versions of the back-projected films; the Ian Eames original with animated clocks, used in the Seventies and on the 1987-89 tour, and Storm Thorgerson's 1994 update, starting with Eames clocks but then using new computer animation.

For concerts without the whole *Dark Side...* suite, 'Breathe', 'Time' and 'Breathe Reprise' were played as one piece.

 ### GREAT GIG IN THE SKY
For the first time the credits read "Wright/ Vocal composition by Clare Torry". As on *Delicate Sound...*, her role is reprised by all three backing vocalists; first Sam Brown, then Durga McBroom, then Claudia Fontaine.

Again, the DVD includes two concert films. The first is of waves, from the *Crystal Voyager* movie (see under 'Echoes'), the other, showing some rather strange animated fish, was used on only a few 1994 dates, before the former was returned to use.

 ### MONEY
Recorded mainly at Festa Nazionale dell'Unita, Modena, September 17, with part of Dick Parry's saxophone solo from an Earls Court show.

The DVD includes both the 1987 and 1994 backing films. The former is very similar to, if not the same as, that used in the 1970, with footage of luxury goods and copies of *Dark Side...* being mass produced. The latter is a strange Strom Thorgerson affair, with a comic alien.

 ### US AND THEM
Again, there are two backing films, the 1987 version (using material from the Seventies original) and a 1994 Storm Thorgerson version, updating the Seventies version. Where the *Dark Side...* suite was not performed, 'Great Gig...', 'Us And Them' and 'Money' would often be

played, usually in that order, during the band's second set.

 ANY COLOUR YOU LIKE

The oil-slide light effects are by Peter Wynne-Wilson, who rejoined the band for the tour, having being their lighting engineer in 1966/67, when he was paid a percentage, as though he was a band member. Before that, he'd run the lighting at the UFO Club. On nights when *Dark Side...* wasn't performed, he did the same thing for 'Astronomy Domine'.

 BRAIN DAMAGE

The backing film, directed by Caroline Wright, shows a selection of contemporary and historical world leaders and other politicians, intercut with scenes of war.

 ECLIPSE

In the backing film, the Sun *is* eclipsed by the Moon.

 WISH YOU WERE HERE

Sometimes performed straight after *Dark Side...*, and sometimes as the first encore, this was recorded in Rome on September 20.

 COMFORTABLY NUMB

The encore comprised three songs. Jon Carin, Guy Pratt and Richard Wright again sing Roger Waters' role as a team.

The new, bigger mirror ball is seen in all its glory.

 RUN LIKE HELL

Guy Pratt again sings, or rather shouts, his "send you back to London..." line.

 SOUNDSCAPE

(Gilmour/Wright/Mason)
(Cassette only)

A 22-minute section of a longer ambient piece used as a preamble to the concerts, where it started quietly, with the house lights still up, as the audience took their seats, usually oblivious to it and grew slowly in volume as the house lights were finally lowered. It featured the sounds of insects and birds, church bells, a lawnmower, aeroplanes passing overhead and an extract of 'Cluster One'. Though included on the now-withdrawn cassette version of *P*U*L*S*E*, it has been released in full nowhere else. That said, a six-minute extract is used on the DVD, uncredited, as the backing soundtrack for the "photo gallery".

DVD EXTRAS

 CONCERT FILMS

Tracks: Shine On You Crazy Diamond; Learning To Fly; High Hopes; Speak To Me (2); On The Run; Time (2); The Great Gig In The Sky (2); Money (2); Us And Them (2); Brain Damage; Eclipse

All the backing films used during the concerts, including second versions for some songs, each synchronised with the relevant part of the audio recording (described above).

ROCK AND ROLL HALL OF FAME INDUCTION CEREMONY

The members of Pink Floyd, including Syd Barrett and Roger Waters, were inducted into the Rock and Roll Hall of Fame at the Waldorf Astoria Hotel, New York, on January 17, 1996. Included on the DVD was an edited version of the induction speech by The Smashing Pumpkins' Billy Corgan; the acceptance by David Gilmour, Nick Mason and Richard Wright; and a rendition of 'Wish You Were Here', by Gilmour, Wright and Corgan. Barrett (of course) and Waters did not attend.

BOOTLEGGING THE BOOTLEGGERS

Four tracks ('What Do You Want From Me', 'On The Turning Away', 'Poles Apart', 'Marooned') performed occasionally on the tour, as filmed by bootleggers, but with soundboard recordings added.

PROMO VIDEOS

The promo videos for 'Learning To Fly' and 'Take It Back'.

SAY GOODBYE TO LIFE AS WE KNOW IT

Behind-the-scenes footage filmed by the road crew and band members' families (presumably, the person asking Nick Mason for a kiss isn't a roadie).

OTHER

The DVD also included:

- a photo gallery
- album over art
- the 1995 television advert for the album
- maps of tour venues
- a list of concert dates
- engineering drawings of the stage sets

IS THERE ANYBODY OUT THERE? THE WALL LIVE 1980-81

Boxed edition released 18 April 2000 as EMI 5 23562 2
Regular CD: EMI 24075 2
UK Chart: No. 15

Tracks: MC: Atmos; In The Flesh?; The Thin Ice; Another Brick In The Wall - Part 1; The Happiest Days Of Our Lives; Another Brick In The Wall - Part 2; Mother; Goodbye Blue Sky; Empty Spaces; What Shall We Do Now?; Young Lust; One Of My Turns; Don't Leave Me Now; Another Brick In The Wall - Part 3; The Last Few Bricks; Goodbye Cruel World; Hey You; Is There Anybody Out There?; Nobody Home; Vera; Bring The Boys Back Home; Comfortably Numb; The Show Must Go On; MC: Atmos; In The Flesh; Run Like Hell; Waiting For The Worms; Stop; The Trial; Outside The Wall

After many years, and difficult negotiations between the post-split camps, the band finally acquiesced to fans' requests to release a live recording of *The Wall* concerts.

Initial copies came in a slip-case, packaged as a hard-back, 68-page book, 14x25cm, with a CD in a pocket inside each cover. It featured interviews, conducted by Nick Sedgewick, with each of the four band members (Wright is endearingly frank about the breakdown of his relationship with Waters, his departure from the band, his failure to contribute to writing, and his "anger and hurt"), Gerald Scarfe, stage designers

Mark Fisher and Jonathan Park and lastly James Guthrie, who worked at the concert as the sound mixer. Later editions were packaged in a regular double CD jewel-case, with interviews and artwork in not one, but two really fat booklets.

The recordings are from a mix of different dates in August 1980 and June 1981, all at Earls Court, London, and therefore feature both Snowy White and Andy Roberts. Many of the songs were longer than the album versions, with extended intros and outros, and longer or additional guitar and keyboard solos (some taken by members of the surrogate band). 'The Show Must Go On' included the lyrics which had been excised from the studio version for reasons of brevity,

The original USA release titled the two versions of 'MC: Atmos' as the more descriptive 'Master Of Ceremonies'; later releases there changed this to be in line with those in the rest of the world.

For a track-by-track analysis, story description, and full line-up, see the entry for *The Wall*.

ECHOES:
THE BEST OF PINK FLOYD

Released 5 November 2001
as EMI 5 36111 2
UK Chart: #2, recharted 2005 (No. 19)

Tracks: Astronomy Domine; See Emily Play; The Happiest Days Of Our Lives; Another Brick In The Wall (Part 2); Echoes; Hey You;

Marooned; The Great Gig In The Sky; Set The Controls For The Heart Of The Sun; Money; Keep Talking; Sheep; Sorrow; Shine On You Crazy Diamond (Parts 1-7); Time; The Fletcher Memorial Home; Comfortably Numb; When The Tigers Broke Free; One Of These Days; Us And Them; Learning to Fly; Arnold Layne; Wish You Were Here; Jug Band Blues; High Hopes; Bike

Pink Floyd surprised fans once again with this compilation. Some (but not all, as is often claimed) of the tracks segue, such as 'See Emily Play' into 'The Happiest Days of Our Lives' and 'Sheep' into 'Sorrow'; the work of James Guthrie, who is credited, with Pink Floyd, with co-producing the compilation. Many of them are abridged, such as the 16½ minute 'Echoes', 'Sheep', which fades out after 9¾ minutes and the 17½ minute 'Shine On You Crazy Diamond (Parts 1-7)'. Even 'Marooned' is cut by over half, to just a tad over two minutes. Conversely, 'Comfortably Numb' is stretched, at its start, by the inclusion of material previously indexed as the tail end of 'Bring The Boys Back Home'. The running order is far from chronological.

There is nothing from *More*, *Ummagumma*, *Atom Heart Mother* (though David Gilmour had reputedly wanted to include 'Fat Old Son') or *Obscured By Clouds*, but there are three tracks each from *Piper...* and *The Division Bell* and four each from *Dark Side...* and *The Wall*. The artwork was again by Storm Thorgerson.

The CDs came in a slim-line double jewel case inside a cardboard sleeve, each face and the centre-spread having different Thorgerson designs, using a great many motifs from throughout the band's career, such as the red scarf from *Wish You Were Here* and the dancers from *...Dance Songs*, alongside the inevitable pigs and prisms.

THE PINK FLOYD AND SYD BARRETT STORY

Released 24 March 2003
as Direct Video DVDUK009D
"Definitive Edition" released 6 February
2006 as Direct Video DVDSD0002D

Unlike many of the truly awful, cheaply compiled Pink Floyd documentary DVDs which have flooded the market in recent years, this made-for-BBC-television documentary is of commendable quality and has noteworthy content. Narrated by Kirsty Wark, it should really be called "The Syd Barrett Story": though it features specially, and separately, recorded interviews with David Gilmour, Nick Mason, Roger Waters, Richard Wright, they're all about the Madcap. All are frank, and deeply touching. Other interviewees are early band member Bob Klose, Peter Jenner, Syd Barrett's first girlfriend, Libby Chisman, his post-Floyd flatmate Duggie Fields and collaborators including Mike Leonard (college tutor to some of the band, he was also their landlord and musical collaborator), Aubrey 'Po' Powell, Mick Rock and Jerry Shirley. Robyn Hitchcock performs 'Dominoes' and 'It Is Obvious' and Blur's Graham Coxon plays 'Love You' (though only extracts are seen, the full performances are included as extras).

Of special note is the included snatch of the unreleased first Pink Floyd demo, 'King Bee', and one of his last songs with Pink Floyd, 'Vegetable Man', in much better quality than the more familiar bootlegged versions, and so holding out some hope for an eventual

official release. There's also documentary footage of the as-yet unsigned band jamming for an episode of science programme *Tomorrow's World*, about Mike Leonard's experimental light show.

In one of the other extras, Gilmour picks up an acoustic guitar and demonstrates how he came to compose the riff for 'Wish You Were Here'. A longer segment of the Waters interview is another extra.

A twin-DVD "Definitive Edition" set was released in 2006, with even longer versions of the interviews with Gilmour, Mason and Wright (about half an hour each), a quiz, a brief tour of Abbey Road Studios (viewable only when the quiz is completed; "Norman Smith" is the answer accepted for the question about the producer of their first two singles; none of the options given mentions Joe Boyd), and more.

CLASSIC ALBUMS: PINK FLOYD – THE MAKING OF THE DARK SIDE OF THE MOON

DVD released August 2003
as Eagle Rock Entertainment EREDV329

Hot on the heels of the above, 2003 saw another notable documentary, directed by Matthew Longfellow, appear on DVD. It was again made with the involvement of all four band members. Without their consent, the opportunity to hear Alan Parsons explaining the album's make-up by playing individual tracks from the master tape would surely not have been possible. Indeed, "special thanks" are credited to Steve O'Rourke and Mark Fenwick (Roger Waters' post-Floyd manager) and the whole thing is a co-production with, and copyright to, Pink Floyd Music Limited.

All four musicians are interviewed, individually, as are Parsons, Chris Thomas, Storm Thorgerson, former Columbia Records chairman Bhaskar Menon, and music journalists. David Gilmour, Roger Waters and Richard Wright each recreate and explain their contributions and demos, live recordings and rehearsal tales are heard.

On top of the 50-minute programme, extra features totalling over half-an-hour are included, with fuller versions of some of the performances and longer interview clips.

In short, it's exemplary.

LIVE8

DVD released: November 7 2005
as EMI 3 41668 9

Tracks: Speak To Me; Breathe; Money; Wish You Were Here; Comfortably Numb

On July 2, 2005, the unthinkable happened: Pink Floyd performed live, with Roger Waters back in the line-up, alongside David Gilmour, Nick Mason and Richard Wright for the first

time since the last of *The Wall* concerts. (There had been an earlier rapprochement, when Mason made guest appearances at two of Waters' concerts at Wembley Arena, London, in June 2002.)

At the behest of Bob Geldof, Waters had telephoned Gilmour, to the latter's surprise, to suggest a one-off reunion for the purpose of supporting the *Make Poverty History* campaign and the Global Call for Action Against Poverty, by performing at the London Live8 concert in Hyde Park. After a day for consideration Gilmour agreed, saying, "Any squabbles Roger and the band have had in the past are so petty in this context, and if re-forming for this concert will help focus attention then it's got to be worthwhile". He later described the performance as "a bit like sleeping with your ex-wife".

Although invited, Guy Pratt understandably opted not to rejoin Pink Floyd, perhaps thinking that one bass player would be sufficient, and instead contributed from Germany, as part of Roxy Music. Largely unseen and uncredited, Tim Renwick provided extra guitar (notably in the intro to 'Wish You Were Here') and bass, and Jon Carin keyboards. Dick Parry performed on the aptly chosen 'Money' (also used for the DVD's menu) and Carol Kenyon sang backing vocals on 'Comfortably Numb'.

Later that year, their entire performance was included on a four-DVD compilation from the event, with DTS and Dolby 5.1 soundtracks and a widescreen format.

Even more remarkable was the inclusion of an eight-minute extra feature, *Pink Floyd Rehearsals*, including interviews with all four band members, recorded during rehearsals, and a compete run-through of 'Wish You Were Here', followed by several attempts by David Gilmour and Roger Waters to teach Nick Mason the ending. Band members are also seen in the *Backstage At Hyde Park* extra, albeit only onstage during 'Hey Jude', the concert's (and Paul McCartney's) closing number, and nowhere near microphones at that.

For the first time in its history, they performed 'Breathe' with 'Breathe (Reprise)' appended as an extra verse.

OVERSEAS COMPILATIONS

A few of the many compilations released around the globe are of special interest because they offer fans the chance to obtain rare recordings without paying over the odds for original singles. Those on CD also offer, of course, better quality. The sooner Pink Floyd allow EMI to collect these, and other, rare tracks and release them properly, the happier fans will be.

MASTERS OF ROCK VOL. 1

Harvest 1 C 054-04 299, released: 1974

Tracks: Chapter 24; Mathilda Mother (sic); Arnold Layne; Candy And A Currant Bun; Scarecrow; Apples And Oranges; It Would Be So Nice; Paint Box; Julia Dream; See Emily Play.

A now-deleted European, vinyl-only release, once sought after because of its inclusion of some early singles, and for using the mono master of 'Julia Dream' – like some of the other mono sources used, it was remixed here as artificial stereo.

WORKS

Capitol CDP 7 46478 2;
originally Capitol ST 12276,
released: circa 1983

Tracks: One Of These Days; Arnold Layne;
Fearless; Brain Damage/ Eclipse; Set The
Controls For The Heart Of The Sun; See
Emily Play; Several Species Of Small Furry
Animals Gathered Together In A Cave And
Grooving With A Pict; Free Four; Embryo.

Released only in the US, but widely available
in the UK as an import, this "hits"
compilation only goes up to *Dark Side…*,
after which Pink Floyd changed their
Stateside label to Columbia. It is notable for
the re-emergence of the otherwise hard to
obtain 'Embryo' and the inclusion of some
different mixes, especially 'Brain Damage'
and 'Eclipse', which are taken from
quadraphonic masters.

A CD FULL OF SECRETS

Westwood One Vol. 10,
released: circa 1992

Tracks: Candy And A Currant Bun; See Emily
Play; Flaming (US single version); Apples And
Oranges; Paintbox; It Would Be So Nice; Julia
Dream; Point Me At The Sky; Heartbeat,
Pigmeat; Crumbling Land; Come In Number
51, Your Time Is Up; Biding My Time; Money
(1981 dance version); When The Tigers
Broke Free; Not Now John (obscured
version); Terminal Frost (DYOL mix); Run Like
Hell (live version).

Released for radio use only, in the US, and
useful not only because of its relatively wide
availability, but also for including most of the
non-album single sides (except 'Arnold
Layne', the longer version of 'The Hero's
Return' and some live cuts), notably the only
CD versions of the US single mix of 'Flaming'
and the "polite", single version of 'Not Now
John'. It has also been pirated, by a label
claiming to be based in Luxembourg.

The 'dance' version of 'Money' is the version
from *…Great Dance Songs*. The live 'Run
Like Hell' is from the 'On The Turning Away'
single.

PART II
SOLO RECORDINGS

Like their colleagues in bands of similar stature, the members and former members of Pink Floyd have recorded many solo albums. In the case of David Gilmour (at least initially), Nick Mason and Richard Wright, these were either ways of passing the time (and tax exile) between band projects, or extra-curricular dalliances that allowed them to release music incompatible with "The Pink Floyd Sound". However, the solo projects of Syd Barrett (particularly given the involvement of his former band-mates) and, latterly, Roger Waters, give us glimpses of the alternative Pink Floyds which may have existed had fate had different tricks to play.

SYD BARRETT

THE MADCAP LAUGHS

Released: 3 January 1970
as Harvest SHVL 765
First CD: Harvest CDP 7 46607 2
Extended remaster: Harvest 8 28906 2;
8 28906 2; 3 May 1994
Tracks: Terrapin; No Good Trying; Love You; No Man's Land; Dark Globe; Here I Go; Octopus; Golden Hair; Long Gone; She Took A Long Cold Look; Feel; If It's In You; Late Night; bonus tracks: Octopus (Takes 1 & 2); It's No Good Trying (Take 5); Love You (Take 1); Love You (Take 3); She Took A Long Cold Look At Me (Take 4); Golden Hair (Take 5)

Variously produced by Dave Gilmour and Roger Waters, Malcolm Jones, Dave Gilmour and Syd Barrett, and Peter Jenner. Only later CD issues contained the bonus tracks.

'Golden Hair' is a poem by James Joyce, set to music by Barrett, and was the B-side of Barrett's only single, 'Octopus' (Harvest HAR 5009).
The cover shows Barrett's room at the flat he shared with Duggie Fields, with striped floorboards he painted himself.

BARRETT

Released 14 November 1970 as
Harvest SHSP 4007
First CD: Harvest CDP 7 466606 2
Extended remaster: EMI 8 28907 2;
3 May 1994
Tracks: Baby Lemonade; Love Song; Dominoes; It Is Obvious; Rats; Maisie; Gigolo Aunt; Waving My Arms In The Air/ I Never Lied To You; Wined And Dined; Wolfpack; Effervescing Elephant; bonus tracks: Baby Lemonade (Take 1); Waving My Arms In The Air (Take 1); I Never Lied To You (Take 1); Love Song (Take 1); Dominoes (Take 1); Dominoes (Take 2); It Is Obvious (Take 2)

Produced by Dave Gilmour. Only later CD issues contained the bonus tracks, but earlier releases credit Richard Wright as co-producer. The first two Syd Barrett solo albums were available, on vinyl only, as the double album 'Syd Barrett' (Harvest SHDW404). The insect paintings on the cover are by Barrett.

THE PEEL SESSION

Released February 1988
as Strange Fruit SFPSCD 043
Tracks: Terrapin; Gigolo Aunt; Effervescing
Elephant; Two Of A Kind; Baby Lemonade

Recorded on February 24, 1970 for John
Peel's BBC Radio 1's *Top Gear* show and
broadcast on May 18, with Jerry Shirley
(drums) and David Gilmour (bass). Produced
by John Walters. Although initially credited to

Syd Barrett, 'Two Of A Kind' turned out to be
a Richard Wright composition. Later reissued
as part of *The Radio One Sessions*
(see below).

OPEL

Released 17 October 1988
as Harvest SHSP 4126
First CD: Harvest CDP 7 91206 2
Extended remaster: Harvest 8 28908 2;
3 May 1994
Tracks: Opel; Clowns & Jugglers (Octopus);
Rats; Golden Hair; Dolly Rocker; Word Song;
Wined & Dined; Swan Lee (Silas Lang);
Birdie Hop; Let's Split; Lanky (Part 1);
Wouldn't You Miss Me (Dark Globe); Milky
Way; Golden Hair (Instrumental); bonus
tracks: Gigolo Aunt (Take 9); It Is Obvious
(Take 3); It Is Obvious (Take 5); Clowns &
Jugglers (Take 1); Late Night (Take 2);
Effervescing Elephant (Take 2)

A compilation of demos, alternate takes and
unreleased material from the first two
albums, with various producers. Only later
CD issues contained the bonus tracks.

OCTOPUS:
THE BEST OF SYD BARRETT

Released in the USA only on
29 May 1992 as Cleopatra Records
CLEO 57712
Tracks: Octopus; Swan Lee (Silas Lang);
Baby Lemonade; Late Night; Wined And
Dined; Golden Hair; Gigolo Aunt; Wolfpack;
It Is Obvious; Lanky (Part 1); No Good Trying;
Clowns & Jugglers; Waving My Arms In The
Air; Opel

A US-only release, with no rarities, although
initial copies came in a cloth bag with a
Syd Barrett badge and photograph.

CRAZY DIAMOND –
THE COMPLETE SYD BARRETT

Released: 26 April 1993
as Harvest CDS 7 81412 2
This three CD box set includes 'The Madcap
Laughs', 'Barrett' and 'Opel', each with
bonus tracks, plus a 24-page booklet.
The extended discs were later released
individually, as listed above.

THE BEST OF SYD BARRETT:
WOULDN'T YOU MISS ME?

Released 16 April 2001
as EMI 5 32320 2
Tracks: Octopus; Late Night; Terrapin; Swan
Lee (Silas Lang); Wolfpack; Golden Hair;
Here I Go; Long Gone; No Good Trying; Opel;
Baby Lemonade; Gigolo Aunt; Dominoes;
Wouldn't You Miss Me (Dark Globe); Wined
And Dined; Effervescing Elephant; Waving My
Arms In The Air; I Never Lied To You; Love
Song; Two Of A Kind; Bob Dylan Blues;
Golden Hair (Instrumental)

To entice fans who already owned the original albums, this compilation featured 'Bob Dylan Blues', a previously unreleased demo recording from February 1970, the master tape of which had been kept by its producer, David Gilmour, in his private collection.

The recording of 'Two Of A Kind was from the 1970 John Peel session.

THE RADIO ONE SESSIONS

Released 29 March 2004
as Strange Fruit SFRSCD127
Tracks: Terrapin; Gigolo Aunt; Baby Lemonade; Effervescing Elephant; Two Of A Kind; Baby Lemonade; Dominoes; Love Song

Features the complete Peel Sessions recordings, as released in 1988, plus three previously unreleased songs recorded solo, for a Bob Harris/ BBC Radio 1 show of 16 February 1971. The latter are lifted from a bootleg, since the BBC no longer have the original tapes.

DAVID GILMOUR

Jokers Wild

UNTITLED
(as Jokers Wild)

RSLP 007, private pressing of
50 copies, recorded circa 1965
Tracks: Why Do Fools Fall In Love; Walk Like A Man; Don't Ask Me (What I Say); Big Girls Don't Cry; Beautiful Delilah

Prior to joining Pink Floyd, David Gilmour cut a five track, one-sided album with his band Jokers Wild, at Regent Sound in Denmark Street, London. Only 40 or 50 copies were pressed, for family and friends. All the songs are soul standards, and two, 'Don't Ask Me' and 'Why Do Fools Fall In Love', were used on a 7" single (RSR 0031), which had an equally limited run. In 1994, a copy sold for over £800, but readers can avoid the expense by visiting the British Library's National Sound Archive in London, where a tape-recording of the album can be heard by personal callers who quote reference "C-625/1".

DAVID GILMOUR

Released 25 May 1978
as Harvest SHVL 817
Remaster: EMI 3 70843 2;
August 14, 2006
Tracks: Mihalis; There's No Way Out Of Here;
Cry From The Street; So Far Away; Short And
Sweet; Raise My Rent; No Way; Definitely; I
Can't Breathe Anymore

In 1978, while Waters prepared demos of
The Wall and *Pros And Cons Of Hitch Hiking*,
Gilmour worked on his first proper solo
album with Rick Wills and Willie Wilson,
respectively the bassist and drummer from
his various bands before joining Pink Floyd.
The trio returned to France for the recording
sessions, produced by David Gilmour, which
took place at Superbear Studios. Backing
vocals on 'There's No Way Out Of Here' and
'So Far Away' were provided by Debbie Doss,
Shirley Roden and Carlena Williams. Mick
Weaver played piano on the latter.

The album's only single, an edit of 'There's
No Way Out Of Here' (Harvest HAR 5167),
made no impact on the charts. The song had
originally appeared on the Gilmour-produced
Unicorn album *Too Many Crooks* as 'No Way
Out Of Here'. 'Short And Sweet' was co-
written with Roy Harper for his *Unknown
Soldier* album, on which Gilmour played.

A half-hour promotional video for the album,
recorded live, but in a studio, featured Wills
and Wilson, plus Gilmour's brother Mark on
rhythm guitar, and included 'There's No Way

Out Of Here', 'So Far Away', 'No Way',
'I Can't Breathe Anymore' and 'Mihalis'.
It has never been officially released.

ABOUT FACE

Released: March 5 1984
as Harvest SHSP 24-0079-1
First CD: Harvest CDP 7 46031 2
Remaster: EMI 3 70842 2
Tracks: Until We Sleep; Murder; Love On The
Air; Blue Light; Out Of The Blue; All Lovers
Are Deranged; You Know I'm Right; Cruise;
Let's Get Metaphysical; Near The End

About Face, produced by Bob Ezrin and
Gilmour, was the latter's response to the
hiatus in Pink Floyd work after *The Final Cut*.
Although Pete Townshend contributed the
lyrics of 'Love On The Air' and 'All Lovers Are
Deranged', Gilmour wrote everything else
and his songs are certainly up to scratch,
making it hard to understand why he has
needed so much help on subsequent Floyd
albums. He assembled a band for a seventy-
odd date tour of Europe and America, but
the audiences were not of Pink Floyd
proportions.

'Blue Light' was issued as an edited 7" and
as a 12" single, both backed by 'Cruise'
(Harvest HAR 5226). In the USA, there was
another 12", with vocal and instrumental
remixes by François Kevorkian and Frank
Filipetti (Columbia 44-04983). This was only
released in the UK as a DJ promo (Harvest
DG1).

The follow-up, 'Love On The Air'/ 'Let's Get Metaphysical' was put out in 7" and picture disc formats, the latter in the outline of a valve radio, backed with a picture of David Gilmour (Harvest HAR 5229).

The album was released in a remastered form in 2006, with a slightly longer running time, caused in part by a much longer fade-out on the final track.

Another piece of music written for the album was not used by Gilmour. He asked Townshend and, separately, Roy Harper, to supply lyrics, but felt that those provided were not messages to which he could relate. Harper subsequently used the tune, with his lyrics, as 'Hope', on his 1985 album with Jimmy Page, *Whatever Happened To Jugula?* (Science Friction HUCD032). Townshend used it with his as 'White City Fighting', on which Gilmour plays, and which has a markedly faster tempo, on his 1984 album *White City: A Novel* (SPV Records, SPV97692CD).

DAVID GILMOUR (film)

Released in the USA only in 1984 as CBS Fox 7078
Tracks: Until We Sleep; All Lovers Are Deranged; There's No Way Out Of Here; Short And Sweet; Run Like Hell; Out Of The Blue; Blue Light; Murder; Comfortably Numb; bonus tracks: Blue Light; All Lovers Are Deranged; Beyond The Floyd

David Gilmour promoted *About Face* with a couple of television appearances, including the Jools Holland-presented *The Tube*, and a three-month tour of Western Europe and the USA – as much as anything to test the waters of a possible solo career, since Roger Waters had not yet left Pink Floyd, but equally showed no inclination to produce another Floyd album. His touring band was Mick Ralphs (guitars), Mickey Feat (bass), Raf Ravenscroft (saxophone), Gregg Dechart (keyboards), Chris Slade (drums) and Jodi Linscott (percussion). Ticket sales were reportedly poor.

At one of the London shows, the support band annoyed Gilmour by reading out Syd Barrett's home address, so, at a subsequent concert in Birmingham, he invited The Dream Academy to support him. That band's leader, Nick Laird Clowes, introduced their stand-in bassist to Gilmour. That bassist was Guy Pratt, and both men were to play a significant part in later Pink Floyd work.

The April 30, 1984 show, at London's Hammersmith Odeon, was filmed for this USA-only video release, directed by Michael Hurll and complete with guest appearances by Roy Harper duetting on 'Short And Sweet' and adding percussion to 'Comfortably Numb'. The latter also featured an unemployed drummer called Nick Mason.

As a bonus, the promo videos for 'Blue Light' and 'All Lovers Are Deranged' were included, as was a 30-minute documentary, *Beyond The Floyd*, with backstage footage and interviews.

The film has never been released as a DVD, but is high on fans' wish-lists.

DEEP END LIVE

Released as Atco 90553
on October 1986 in the USA
Reissued by Eel Pie in 2005
Tracks (original): Barefootin'; After The Fire; Behind Blue Eyes; Stop Hurting People; I'm One; I Put A Spell On You; Save It For Later;

Pinball Wizard; Little Is Enough; Eyesight To The Blind; tracks (2005 reissue): Mary Anne With The Shaky Hand; Won't Get Fooled Again; A Little Is Enough; Secondhand Love; That's Alright Mama; Behind Blue Eyes; The Shout; Harlem Shuffle; Barefootin'; After The Fire; Love On The Air; Midnight Lover; Blue Light; I Put A Spell On You; I'm One; Driftin'; Magic Bus; Save It For Later; Eyesight To The Blind; Walkin'; Stop Hurting People; The Sea Refuses No River; Boogie Stop Shuffle; Face The Face; Pinball Wizard; Give Blood; Night Train

After making a guest appearance on Pete Townshend's *White City: A Novel*, David Gilmour worked with Townshend in Deep End, a short-lived band who performed a handful of benefit concerts for Townshend's "Double O" charity, including another appearance on *The Tube*, two nights at The Brixton Academy, London (an advertised third night was cancelled) and at MIDEM, a music industry trade fair in Cannes. The group included Simon Phillips (drums), Chucho Merchan (bass), Jody Linscott (percussion), John 'Rabbit' Bundrick (keyboard), Peter Hope Evans (harmonica), backing vocalists, and the five-piece "Kick Horns" brass section. Townshend's daughter Emma was guest vocalist on some numbers. The music was mostly Townshend's, but Gilmour's playing contribution was considerable, and his 'Love On The Air' and 'Blue Light' were featured.

A live album, recorded in Brixton on 2 November 1985, was released in the USA and Canada in 1986, featuring ten tracks, and in 2005, the complete concert was issued on a double-CD in Townshend's "Signature" series, as *Live > Brixton Academy 1985*. The original album has also been reissued on CD.

AMNESTY INTERNATIONAL'S BIG 30

Released 1992
as Video Collection VC6198
Renowned human rights organisation Amnesty International celebrated its 30th anniversary in 1991, with a concert recorded on December 13 & 15 at Central Television's Nottingham Studios, and broadcast on December 28. David Gilmour and Jools Holland acted as musical directors and Gilmour put together the house band, which included Tim Renwick, Gary Wallis, Pino Palladino, Jon Carin, Jody Linscott, Sam Brown, Margo Buchanan, a horn section and others.

Originally released as a stand-alone home video cassette, the whole show is now available on DVD, as part of the four-disc *The Secret Policeman's Ball – The Complete Edition* set (ILC DVD 2254; released 2002). (The set also includes *The Secret*

Policeman's Third Ball, filmed over four nights in March 1987, with Gilmour in Kate Bush's band for 'Running Up That Hill', along with Tony Franklin (bass), Kevin McAlea (keyboards) and Stuart Elliot (drums). Nick Mason also performed, but, though credited, is not seen in the film.)

As a musical director, Gilmour performed with a number of guest artists:

I CAN'T TURN YOU LOOSE
With Tom Jones. Gilmour subsequently made guest appearances at some of Jones' concerts.

HARD TO HANDLE
Sung by Andrew Strong from *The Commitments*, an Alan Parker film.

HEY JOE
With Seal. Gilmour does Hendrix; for whom he had once worked as a roadie and sound engineer; with whom Pink Floyd toured in 1967; and who lent Pink Floyd equipment after theirs was stolen in America.

WHAT'S GOING ON
With Daryl Hall, formerly of Hall & Oates.

BIG BOTTOM
Gilmour gets to play bass with spoof heavy metal band Spinal Tap.

ON THE TURNING AWAY
Gilmour's own contribution is, annoyingly, faded as the final solo starts.

KISS
With Tom Jones again, to close the show, joined by many other cast members and providing a wonderful opportunity to hear Gilmour imitating Prince's guitar playing, but sadly faded after the first solo.

THE COLOURS OF INFINITY

Video released 1994
as Prism Leisure Video PLATV 956

In 1994, David Gilmour recorded a soundtrack for this 53-minute film (released in 1995), about fractal geometry, at the behest of another friend from his Cambridge schooldays, the director Nigel Lesmoir-Gordon. Gordon had come to the attention of Floyd fans when a 12-minute silent home movie he had taken, showing a young Syd Barrett tripping on magic mushrooms, was released on DVD as the exploitative *Syd's First Trip*. He later directed and appeared in the Barrett-inspired *Remember A Day* movie.

The fractal film was co-written and presented by Arthur C. Clarke. Interesting though it is, for repeated enjoyment, it would have been good to be able to listen to a separate music track, and watch the fractals, without the talking heads. It's mostly guitar-based, but one synthesiser segment sounds very reminiscent of 'On The Run'. Storm Thorgerson is given "special thanks" in the closing credits.

Though originally released on home video, the programme was later available as a bonus "region-free" DVD included with the soft-back book *The Colours Of Infinity, The Beauty And The Power Of Fractal* by Arthur C Clarke & others (ISBN: 978-1-904555-05-6), published in the UK by Clear Press, in 2004. The book includes a full transcript of the film, and a chapter about its making, including a brief reference to Gilmour's involvement.

DAVID GILMOUR IN CONCERT

DVD released 21 October 2002
as EMI 492958 9

Tracks: Shine On You Crazy Diamond (Parts 1 - 5); Terrapin; Fat Old Sun; Coming Back To Life; High Hopes; Je crois entendre encore, Smile; Wish You Were Here; Comfortably Numb (with Wyatt); Dimming Of The Day (Thompson); Shine On You Crazy Diamond (Parts 6 - 8); A Great Day For Freedom; Hushabye Mountain; bonus tracks: Dominoes; Breakthrough; Comfortably Numb

Filmed as part of Robert Wyatt's *Meltdown* Festival at the Royal Festival Hall on June 21, 2001, a relaxed and happy Gilmour performs a selection of his own material and cover versions, including a confident and bluesy solo rendition of 'Shine On...', joined only by Dick Parry on sax at the end: perfect, but for the hollerin' idiot in the audience.

The rest of Gilmour's band was Neill MacColl (guitars, backing vocals), Michael Kamen (piano, cor anglais), Chucho Merchan (double bass), Caroline Dale (cello), Nic France (drums).

Wyatt made a guest appearance, to sing, or occasionally speak, Waters' part on 'Comfortably Numb' from a position in the stalls. 'Je crois entendre encore' (that's the title, not something performed after the main event!) is an aria by Georges Bizet, from his 1863 opera *The Pearl Fishers,* with the libretto by Eugène Cormon and Michel Carré.

It is sung by a tenor in the opera, but Gilmour's version is somewhat higher. 'Dimming Of The Day' is a Sufi devotional song written by Richard Thompson, from his 1975 album *Pour Down Like Silver*. 'Hushabye Mountain' is a lullaby, written by the Sherman Brothers, for the 1968 film *Chitty Chitty Bang Bang*. 'Smile', which featured Aitch McRobbie on harmony vocals, would late appear on Gilmour's *On An Island* album.

The three bonus tracks were filmed at the same venue during a brief run of Gilmour dates (three in London, two in Paris), in January 2002. They use the same band, and feature a guest appearance by a bespectacled Richard Wright, to perform 'Breakthrough' from his *Broken China* album – its only live rendition, and one which shows the choir at their best. Bob Geldof reprises his role in *The Wall* film to sing the Waters part in 'Comfortably Numb', and looks and sounds extremely uncomfortable and uninterested while doing so.

Among the 30 minutes of special features are a performance of Screaming Jay Hawkins' 'I Put A Spell On You', with Jools Holland and Mica Paris (from Gilmour's guest appearance on Holland's *Mister Roadrunner* television show in June, 1992; the band included Pino Palladino [bass], Gilson Lavis [drums] and Matt Irving [keyboards]), 'Don't' (first recorded by Elvis Presley in 1957) from the Leiber & Stoller tribute concert at London's Hammersmith Apollo on June 29, 2001, and a performance of Shakespeare's 'Sonnet 18' ("Shall I compare thee to a summer's day? Thou art more lovely and more temperate…") with a piano accompaniment composed by Michael Kamen. Filmed on the *Astoria*, this later piece was originally prepared as Gilmour's contribution to a February 2002 gala at the Old Vic theatre in aid of the Royal Academy of Dramatic Art.

A "home movie" by Polly Samson records the first rehearsals of 'Je crois entendre encore', with Gilmour on acoustic guitar directing the otherwise unaccompanied choir. The family

dog gets to make a brief appearance, but sadly doesn't perform 'Seamus'.

Other extras are an a capella version of 'High Hopes' backing vocals, by just the show's sizable choir (Sam Brown [leader], Chris Ballin, Pete Brown, Margo Buchanan, Claudia Fontaine, Michelle John Douglas, Sonia Jones, Carol Kenyon, David Laudat, Durga McBroom, Aitch McRobbie, and Beverli Skeete), and a 'Spare Digits' feature – six of the show's guitar solos, seen from an alternative camera angle, concentrating on Gilmour's fretboards.

Finally, a sound tester, for checking that home audio equipment is correctly configured, to make the best of the DVD's Dolby Digital 5.1 surround-sound, is thoughtfully included.

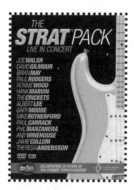

THE STRAT PACK LIVE IN CONCERT

DVD released in 2005 as Eagle Vision EREDV464
A live 2½-hour DVD from a 24 September 2004 benefit concert at London Wembley Arena in aid of Nordoff-Robbins Music Therapy and celebrating the 50th anniversary of the Fender Stratocaster guitar. David Gilmour plays 'Marooned', 'Coming Back To Life' and 'Sorrow' using his famous 1954 Stratocaster, with the 0001 serial number, and participated in the all-star encore, 'Stay With Me', alongside Theresa Anderson, Paul Carrack, Jamie Cullum, Albert Lee, Phil Manzanera, Hank Marvin, Gary Moore, Paul Rodgers, Mike Rutherford, Joe Walsh and

Ronnie Wood. The house band included Andy Fairweather-Low (guitar), Pino Palladino (bass), Ian Thomas (drums) Paul "Wix" Wickens (keyboards), with Margo Buchanan among the backing vocalists. The DVD, directed by Aubrey Powell, has Dolby Digital 5.1, and DTS soundtracks, as well as the regular stereo, all mixed on the *Astoria* by Pink Floyd's sound engineer, Andy Jackson.

ON AN ISLAND

Released 6 March 2006
UK Chart: #1; US Chart: #6
Tracks: Castellorization; On An Island; The Blue; Take A Breath; Red Sky At Night; This Heaven; Then I Close My Eyes; Smile; A Pocketful Of Stones; Where We Start

David Gilmour celebrated his 60th birthday with the release of a new album, produced, mostly on the *Astoria,* by him, Phil Manzanera and Chris Thomas (both of whom also played keyboards).

The original packaging was a twenty-page, CD-sized hard-back book with the CD attached to the inside of the rear cover.

Gilmour wrote all the instrumentals and two of the songs, 'Then I Close My Eyes' and 'Where We Start', and co-wrote the rest with his wife, Polly Samson. As well as guitar, he played Hammond organ, percussion, bass on some tracks (Guy Pratt played on others) and cümbü (a kind of Turkish banjo) on 'Then I Close My Eyes'; and made his saxophone début on 'Red Sky At Night', having learned the instrument alongside his step-son Charlie.

The album had some notable guest appearances. David Crosby and Graham Nash sing harmonies on the title track, which otherwise sounds like an outtake from *The Division Bell*, perhaps because Richard Wright is on Hammond organ. That song and the laid back 'The Blue' feature guitar by a little-known jazz guitarist, Rado Klose, who just happens to have been in the early, pre-

recording contract, line up of Pink Floyd. 'The Blue' also has Jools Holland and Polly Samson on piano. Robert Wyatt contributes cornet to 'Then I Close My Eyes', and Georgie Fame plays Hammond organ on 'This Heaven'. The orchestrations are by celebrated Polish film composer Zbigniew Preisner with the unnamed session orchestra conducted at Abbey Road by Robert Ziegler. Gilmour plays everything on 'Smile', apart from the orchestration, Willie Wilson's drumming and the backing vocals, which are by Samson. Other performers on the album included BJ Cole (dobro), Caroline Dale (cello) , Ged Lynch (drums), Alasdair Malloy (glass harmonica), Leszek Mozdzer (piano), and *Final Cut* contributor Andy Newmark (drums).

There were two UK CD singles; 'On An Island (Edit)' (EMI CDEM688), paired with the album version and 'Smile' (EMI CDEM696), with the bluesy 'Island Jam' (6'33") as the second track. The latter track, produced by Gilmour alone, had Pratt on bass, plus Paul 'Wix' Wickens on Hammond organ and Ged Lynch on drums. In the USA, the 'Jam' was available as a bonus disc with copies purchased from certain retailers.

The album was re-released in November of 2006 with a bonus 53-minute DVD, *Live And In Session*, featuring 'Take A Breath' from David Gilmour's 2006 Royal Albert Hall shows, 'Astronomy Domine' (filmed as part of Gilmour's contribution to the *Live From Abbey Road* television series, but not included in the broadcast) and 'On An Island', 'This Heaven', 'Smile', 'Take A Breath', 'High Hopes' and 'Comfortably Numb' from an *AOL Sessions* webcast from New York. Rick Wright sings the "Waters" verses on the latter song, with no vocal accompaniment, for a change. On 'This Heaven' and 'Smile', Guy Pratt plays an electric upright bass. Limited quantities of this DVD were available for purchase from Gilmour's website, for fans who had already bought the CD.

ARNOLD LAYNE

Released 26 December 2006 as EMI CDEM 717
Tracks: Arnold Layne (featuring David Bowie); Arnold Layne (featuring Richard Wright); Dark Globe

To promote *On An Island*, David Gilmour committed to a short tour of Europe and North America, with a band comprising Richard Wright, Guy Pratt, Jon Carin, Phil Manzanera, and Steve De Stannio on drums (plus Dick Parry, who does not feature on this release). They performed the album in its entirety, with Pink Floyd favourites and obscurities, including, remarkably, the first

ever live outing for *Obscured By Clouds'* 'Wot's... Uh The Deal' and, on one occasion, 'On The Turning Away', which Gilmour started, not having bothered to tell his band that he would be doing so! David Bowie made a surprise guest appearance at two of the Albert Hall shows, to perform 'Arnold Layne' and 'Comfortably Numb'. The former was made available as a download on Christmas Day 2006. The CD single was released the next day, also featuring a Richard Wright performance of the song from the same venue, plus Gilmour's solo rendition of Barrett's 'Dark Globe', recorded "live in Europe in Summer 2006". The recordings were produced by Gilmour.

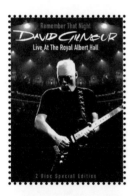

REMEMBER THAT NIGHT

*DVD released 17 September 2007
as EMI 5 04311 9*
*Blu-ray version released
20 November 2007 as EMI 5 04309 9*
Tracks: Speak To Me; Breathe; Time; Breathe (Reprise); Castellorizon; On An Island; The Blue; Red Sky At Night; This Heaven; Then I Close My Eyes; Smile; Take A Breath; A Pocketful Of Stones; Where We Start; Shine On You Crazy Diamond; Fat Old Sun; Coming Back To Life; High Hopes; Echoes; Wish You Were Here; Find The Cost Of Freedom; Arnold Layne; Comfortably Numb. Bonus tracks: Wot's... Uh The Deal; Dominoes; Wearing The Inside; Arnold Layne; Comfortably Numb; Dark Globe; Astronomy Domine; This Is Heaven; Castellorizon; On An Island; The Blue; Take A Breath; High Hopes; Island Jam 2007.

A live DVD, again directed by David Mallet at the Royal Albert Hall, London, over May 29-31, 2006, on the *On An Island* tour. Prior to its release, a five-minute "teaser" was posted to the website in May 2007.

'Find The Cost Of Freedom' is a short Stephen Stills song, which Crosby, Stills, Nash & Young used to close their live album *Four Way Street*. It was performed a capella by Gilmour, with guests David Crosby and Graham Nash, as an encore at several of the *On An Island* shows. At the shows they attended, as here, Crosby and Nash also sang on 'Shine On...', 'On An Island' and 'The Blue', and with Gilmour were jokingly referred to as "Crosby, Gils & Nash". 'Arnold Layne' and 'Comfortably Numb' featured David Bowie's vocals. Robert Wyatt also appeared, on 'Then I Close My Eyes'.

Although Nick Mason made a guest appearance on 'Comfortably Numb' and 'Wish You Were Here' at one show (thereby reuniting the post-Roger Waters Pink Floyd), and appeared in the teaser video, his performances are not included.

A second disc contained bonus material, with five more tracks from the Royal Albert Hall shows: 'Wot's... Uh the Deal', 'Dominoes', 'Wearing The Inside Out', 'Arnold Layne' (with Richard Wright singing) and 'Comfortably Numb' (Wright singing) and five more: 'Castellorizon', 'On An Island', 'The Blue', 'Take A Breath' and 'High Hopes', from a BBC concert appearance at the Mermaid Theatre on March 7, 2006 (also broadcast on BBC Radio 2 and webcast as video).

There were also three documentary features: *Breaking Bread, Drinking Wine*, lasting 46 minutes, follows the tour from the first rehearsals to the final concert in Gdansk, Poland. The others are a "behind the scenes" home movie recorded on the tour's visit to the West Coast of the USA, including some footage filmed by Richard Wright, and *The Making Of 'On An Island'*. Also included were the promo videos for the latter's two singles, 'On An Island' and 'Smile'; Gilmour's rendition of Syd Barrett's 'Dark Globe'; a new version of 'Island Jam'; and 'Astronomy Domine' and 'This Heaven' from the *Live And In Session* DVD, though the latter was a different edit. Altogether, there were over five hours of material.

Disc 2 featured several hidden "Easter egg" extras, including an impromptu acoustic version of 'Echoes', interviews, a dance remix, and a home movie of Gilmour playing the cümbüs. Have fun tracking them down!

A high-resolution Blu-ray version followed the standard DVD release. A promised HD-DVD version appears to have been shelved. 'Wish You Were Here' and 'The Blue' were available as a download-only single.

LIVE IN GDANSK

Released 22 September 2008
2 CD version: EMI 2 35488 2
2 CD + DVD version: EMI 2 35489 2
2 CD + 2 DVD version: EMI 2 35493 2
3 CD + 2 DVD version: EMI 2 35484 2
Plus download-only versions.

Tracks (CDs): Speak To Me; Breathe; Time; Breathe (Reprise); Castellorizon; On An Island; The Blue; Red Sky At Night; This Heaven; Then I Close My Eyes; Smile; Take A Breath; A Pocketful Of Stones; Where We Start; Shine On You Crazy Diamond; Astronomy Domine; Fat Old Sun; High Hopes; Echoes; Wish You Were Here; A Great Day For Freedom; Comfortably Numb.

Recorded on 26 August 2006, the final night of the *On An Island* tour, in the famous shipyard, with an audience of 50,000. The show, a celebration of the 26th Anniversary of the Solidarity movement, was the only one on the tour to feature an orchestra, the 40-piece Polish Baltic Philharmonic Orchestra, conducted by Zbigniew Preisner. Polish jazz pianist Leszek Mozdzer also appeared.

Various permutations were available, adding in turn:

A DVD featuring:
- 15 tracks from the concert: Castellorizon; On An Island; The Blue; Red Sky At Night; This Heaven; Then I Close My Eyes; Smile; Take A Breath; A Pocketful Of Stones; Where We Start; Astronomy Domine; High Hopes; Echoes; A Great Day For Freedom; Comfortably Numb.
- A 36-minute documentary, *Gdansk Diary*.
- A pass-code to download 12 tracks from the 2006 tour: 'Shine On You Crazy Diamond' (Venice, 12 August & Vienna, 31 July); 'Dominoes' (Paris, 15 March); 'The Blue' (Vienna, 31 July); 'Take A Breath' (Munich, 29 July); 'Wish You Were Here' (Glasgow, 27 May); 'Coming Back To Life' (Florence, 2 August); 'Find The Cost Of Freedom' (Manchester, 26 May); 'This Heaven' (Vienna, 31 July); 'Wearing The Inside Out' (Milan, 25 March); 'A Pocketful Of Stones' (Vienna, 31 July); 'Where We Start' (Vienna, 31 July); 'On The Turning Away' (Venice, 12 August). The performance of "Shine On You Crazy Diamond" from Venice features Igor Sklyarov on Glass Harmonica.
A DVD including:
- A 5.1 surround-sound mix of the *On An Island* album.
- Three jams by Gilmour, Wright, Pratt and DiStanislao, with Gilmour credited as composer: Barn Jam 166; Barn Jam 192; Barn Jam 121
- Three tracks from the 2006 Mermaid Theatre show: 'Shine On You Crazy Diamond'; 'Wearing The Inside Out'; 'Comfortably Numb'.
- Two tracks from the AOL sessions: 'On An Island'; 'High Hopes'.
- Three tracks from the *Live At Abbey Road*

show: 'The Blue'; 'Take A Breath'; 'Echoes' (Acoustic).
A CD with the 12 tracks which could be downloaded by purchasers of the lesser sets; plus a wallet of memorabilia

The full set comprises around nine hours of material. The DVDs again include undeclared, "Eater egg" content. A limited-edition five-disc vinyl album was also available, and there are also download-only versions.

In addition to the rendition of 'Remember A Day' in tribute to Wright, Gilmour and band performed 'The Blue' on *Later! Live... With Jools Holland* on BBC2 on 23 September 2008, to promote this release.

CHICAGO – CHANGE THE WORLD

Released August 2009, on-line only
A re-titled cover of the Graham Nash song 'Chicago', released to promote awareness of the plight of Gary McKinnon, a man with autism fighting extradition to the USA. Gilmour sang and played guitar, bass and keyboards. Additional vocals were provided by Chrissie Hynde and Bob Geldof, plus McKinnon himself. Produced by long-time Pink Floyd collaborator Chris Thomas. A video was also posted on-line.

NICK MASON

FICTITIOUS SPORTS

Released: 3 May 1981
as Harvest SHSP 4116
USA CD: Sony WK75070
Tracks: Can't Get My Motor To Start; I Was Wrong; Siam; Hot River; Boo To You Too; Do Ya?; Wervin'; I'm A Mineralist

Nick Mason's first solo effort, released in 1981, was a collaboration with jazz artist Carla Bley. All compositions are by Bley, who co-produced the album with Mason, using her band and her "Grog Kill" studio in New York. The album certainly has much more in

common with her work than Pink Floyd, even if 'Hot River' is a superb Floyd pastiche, with Gilmour's guitar mimicked by Chris Spedding and vocals by Robert Wyatt.

PROFILES
(with Rick Fenn)

Released: 19 August 1985
as Harvest MAF 1
USA CD: Sony A40142
Tracks: Malta; Lie For A Lie; Rhoda; Profiles Parts 1 & 2; Israel; And The Address; Mumbo Jumbo; Zip Code; Black Ice; At The End Of The Day; Profiles Part 3

Profiles is Nick Mason's joint project with Rick Fenn, formerly guitarist for 10cc and Mike Oldfield's band. Mason and Fenn jointly wrote the music and produced the album at their studios, Britannia Row and The Basement respectively. The lyrics to the album's only songs, 'Lie For A Lie' and 'Israel', are by Danny Peyronnel, who also sang on the latter, the only track written without Mason.

Additional contributions came from Mel Collins (saxophone), Craig Pruess (emulator bass on Malta) and Fenn's five-year-old daughter Aja (keyboard intro on 'Malta'). 'Lie For A Lie', with vocals by Maggie Reilly and David Gilmour, was released as a single, backed by 'And The Address' (Harvest HAR 5238). The 12" release (Harvest 12 HAR 5238) also included 'Mumbo Jumbo' and had an extended version of 'Lie…'.

The title track is from the soundtrack to a biographical film about Mason, *Life Could Be A Dream*, which was only ever given a very limited release. It also included a cover of the Crew Cuts' 'Sh'boom', with 10cc's Eric Stewart on vocals, which is sadly not heard on the album.

Mason and Fenn worked together on a number of other projects, including providing the music for a number of television commercials, and the films *Body Contact* (1988), *Cresta Run* (1986), *Tank Malling* (1989, Cineplex Home Entertainment CPX 211; later re-cut as *Beyond Soho*) and *White Of The Eye* (1987, Warner Home Video PEV 37208) – none of the aforesaid are yet on DVD.

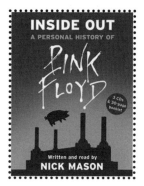

INSIDE OUT
A PERSONAL HISTORY
OF PINK FLOYD

Hardback book published by
Weidenfeld & Nicolson, 2004,
ISBN 978-0-297-84387-0
Updated paperback published
by Phoenix, 2005,
ISBN 978-0-7538-1906-7
Audio book released by Orion,
2 November 2005,
ISBN 978-0-7528-7327-5
Nick Mason's long-awaited and autobiographical history of the band, qualifies – just – for a brief mention here, because the abridged, triple-CD audio version is read by the author himself, with the chapters linked by the ambient sound

effects used by Pink Floyd throughout their history.

The audio CD, and the paperback edition which preceded it, includes an extra chapter, with a post-Live8 update, not in the lavishly illustrated, large format hardback.

ROGER WATERS

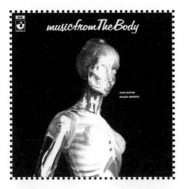

MUSIC FROM THE BODY
(with Ron Geesin)

Released 28 November 1970
as Harvest SHSP 4008
CD: Harvest CDP 7 92548 2
Video: Warner Brothers PES 38196

Tracks: Our Song (Waters/Geesin); Sea Shell And Stone (Waters); Red Stuff Writhe; A Gentle Breeze Blew Through Life; Lick Your Partners; Bridge Passage For Three Plastic Teeth; Chain Of Life (Waters); The Womb Bit (Waters/ Geesin); Embryo Thought; March Past Of The Embryos; More Than Seven Dwarfs In Penis-Land; Dance Of The Red Corpuscles; Body Transport (Waters/ Geesin); Hand Dance - Full Evening Dress; Breathe (Waters); Old Folks Ascension; Bedtime-Dream-Clime; Piddle In Perspex; Embryonic Womb-Walk; Mrs. Throat Goes Walking; Sea Shell And Soft Stone (Waters/ Geesin); Give Birth To A Smile (Waters)

The Body was an innovative (for its time) medical documentary, directed by Roy Battersby, in which Roger Waters narrated

one scene. Music, written by Ron Geesin unless shown, from the film was re-recorded for the "soundtrack" album, produced by the two musicians.

On 'Give Birth To A Smile', Waters is joined by Gilmour, Wright and Mason for an uncredited and often overlooked Pink Floyd performance. Although Waters and Geesin are given equal credit for this album, it is highly unlikely to be filed under 'G' in most record shops.

The video is long unavailable, and there has been no DVD release.

MONSIEUR RENÉ MAGRITTE

DVD Released in the USA
as Image Entertainment ID9292EADVD
A 1978 biography of the surrealist painter René Magritte, directed by Adrian Maben, written and narrated by Edwin Mullins, with incidental music reputedly by Roger Waters. Also sold on video as *Magritte - A Survey of the Entire Career of the Surrealist Master* (Phaidon Press, ISBN 978-0-7148-6020-6)

The music is mostly keyboard noodling, but there's also a guitar solo in strikingly familiar style and a short part of Pink Floyd's 'Obscured By Clouds'. Details are sketchy, and not all of the music may be by Waters. Caveat emptor!

THE PROS AND CONS OF HITCH HIKING

Released: 8 May 1984
as Harvest SHVL 24 0105 1
CD: Harvest CDP 7 46029 2

Tracks: 4.30am (Apparently They Were Travelling Abroad); 4.33am (Running Shoes); 4.37am (Arabs With Knives And West German Skies) 4.39am (For The First Time Today Part 2); 4.41am (Sexual Revolution); 4.47am (The Remains Of Our Love); 4.30am (Go Fishing); 4.56am (For The First Time Today Part 1); 4.58am (Dunroamin, Duncarin, Dunlivin); 5.01am (The Pros And Cons Of Hitch Hiking); 5.06am (Every Strangers Eyes); 5.11am (The Moment Of Clarity)

Waters' first solo album following his departure from Pink Floyd was a development of the demo of another concept offered to the band at the same time as *The Wall,* but rejected as "too personal". All the tracks were "time-stamped", representing the stages of the narrator's dream during one night, including picking up a hitch hiker, meeting Yoko Ono, having an affair in a German hotel, being attacked by terrorists, retiring to the country, being left by his wife and finally, waking to the realisation that his wife is by his side and all is well. Gerald Scarfe's sleeve, featuring well known hard-core porn model Linzi Drew, attracted complaints of sexism, and was censored on some overseas releases.

The album uses Holophonic sound effects. It was recorded with Andy Bown (late of The *Wall* concerts, keyboards and guitars), Ray Cooper (percussion), Michael Kamen (piano, orchestral arrangements and co-production, with Waters), Andy Newmark (drums), David Sanborn (sax) plus backing vocalists Madeline Bell, Katie Kissoon and Doreen Chanter, and horns from Raf Ravenscroft and others. Several actors also had spoken parts, including Ed Bishop, Manning Redwood, Jack Palance and Cherry Vanilla. However, by far the most notable member of the cast was Eric Clapton. Asked by a radio interviewer what Clapton's contribution to the album was, Waters replied with a surprised "he played guitar!" That is something of an understatement, as Clapton's playing is widely regarded as his best for many years, relieved as he was of the burden of leading a band. He performs wonderfully emotional, bluesy passages, including some on Dobro. At around the same time, Waters assisted Clapton on the latter's title music for Stephen Frears' suspense film *The Hit.*

Waters went on the road with Clapton, Kamen, Newmark, Kissoon and Chanter plus Tim Renwick (later to tour with Pink Floyd) and Mel Collins. The whole album was performed with back-projected films (including new Scarfe animation), costumed backing singers and puppets. Audiences also had the chance to hear Clapton play several Floyd classics, such as 'Money', the three short songs from *Wish You Were Here,* 'In The Flesh', 'Hey You' and 'Brain Damage'/'Eclipse'. Clapton was replaced after about twenty dates by Andy Fairweather-Low and Jay Stapley.

'5.01am (The Pros And Cons of Hitch Hiking)' was the album's first single (Harvest HAR 5228), backed by '4.30am (Apparently They Were Travelling Abroad)'. The 12" version (Harvest 12 HAR 5228) also included '4.33am (Running Shoes)' and an extended version of '5.01am (The Pros And Cons Of Hitch Hiking)', with an alternative Eric Clapton guitar solo and extra saxophone.

A second single, '5.06am (Every Strangers Eyes)' (Harvest HAR 5230), backed by

'4.39am (For The First Time Today Part 1)', was very hard to find and is something of a collectors' item.

WHEN THE WIND BLOWS

Released: 30 October 1986
as Virgin CDV2406
DVD: Channel 4 DVD C4DVD10007;
26 September 2005
Tracks: The Russian Missile; Towers Of Faith; Hilda's Dream; The American Bomber; The Anderson Shelter; The British Submarine; The Attack; The Fall Out; Hilda's Hair; Folded Flags

Waters wrote and produced the score of the animated feature film version of Raymond Briggs' graphic novel, directed by Jimmy T. Murakami, with lead characters voiced by Peggy Ashcroft and John Mills. The first half of the album is by other artists.

The score, indexed on CD as one track, is all-instrumental, apart from 'Towers Of Faith' and 'Folded Flags'. The former, a duet with Clare Torry, is not heard in the movie (and is not on the DVD), but was intended to be played in the auditorium as the lights went down, while the latter is a duet between Waters and Paul Carrack. The album credits the recording to "Roger Waters And The Bleeding Heart Band", which included Jay Stapley and Mel Collins, plus new faces Matt Irving and Nick Glennie Smith (both on keyboards), John Linwood (programming), Freddie Krc (drums) and John Gordon (bass).

The DVD of the 89-minute film has Dolby Digital stereo but no surround-sound, and includes a contemporary, 25-minute "Making Of" documentary and a new, 14-minute interview with Briggs.

RADIO KAOS

Released: 15 June 1987
as Harvest KAOS 1
CD: EMI CDP 7 46865 2
Tracks: Radio Waves; Who Needs Information; Me Or Him; The Powers That Be; Sunset Strip; Home; Four Minutes; The Tide Is Turning (After Live Aid)

Radio KAOS had a very 1980s sound, which Waters has since regretted, but is still a powerful album. Its complicated plot required an explanation to be included in the sleeve notes; telling the unlikely tale of Billy, a telepathic paraplegic with the ability to communicate by telephone and computer. Eventually, Billy simulates a nuclear war in order to frighten the world into disarmament. Waters' story also includes attacks on "market forces" and the way in which the fact that "information is power" disenfranchises so many people. Even so, the album ends on a high note, which, as its subtitle suggests, was written the day after the Live Aid concerts, to convey Waters' hopes for the future.

Co-produced with keyboard player Ian Ritchie (and Nick Griffiths on two tracks), *Radio KAOS* was recorded by a basic band of Andy Fairweather-Low, Mel Collins, Jay Stapley and

Graham Broad (drums) with many others contributing, including vocals by Paul Carrack, Clare Torry, Vicky Brown and the Pontarddulais Male Voice Choir. 'The Powers That Be' was performed by most of the line up that recorded the *When The Wind Blows* score, betraying its ancestry. The tracks were linked by conversations between Billy's BBC Micro computer-generated voice and DJ Jim Ladd. In America, radio stations were issued with a promotional LP from which most of the dialogue between Jim Ladd and Billy had been removed.

The first single, 'Radio Waves (7" version)' (EMI EM 6) was backed by 'Going To Live In LA', a demo of a track not used on *Radio KAOS*. The 12" and CD singles had an additional re-mix of 'Radio Waves'. The second single, 'The Tide Is Turning' (EMI EM 37), boasted a "live" version of 'Money'; in reality a home studio recording with dubbed-on audience – Waters' bitter comment on his former band's continued success. The 12" and CD versions also included 'Get Back To Radio', also a demo not used on *Radio KAOS*. Another non-album track, 'Molly's Song', was featured on the US single 'Who Needs Information' (Columbia 38-07617) after being performed as part of the *KAOS* concerts.

Waters followed the album with a video EP, directed by Willie Smax, featuring promo clips for 'Radio Waves'; 'Sunset Strip'; 'Four Minutes' and 'The Tide Is Turning'. A subsequent reissue (Music Club MC 2128) omitted the explanatory liner notes of the original. There has been no DVD issue.

Both Carrack (playing keyboards and singing) and Ladd joined the basic band plus Chanter and Kissoon on a tour to promote the album. The shows, with additional *KAOS* material and Pink Floyd songs interspersed, were presented in the format of a radio show, with the band playing songs introduced by a DJ. During the interval, fans could "phone-in" from a booth in the auditorium and interview Waters. On some nights Waters would be gigging in one American town while Pink

Floyd played some of the same songs in another. A promised live album from the tour never materialised.

THE WALL LIVE IN BERLIN

Released 17 September 1990 as Mercury 846 611 2 DVD released on 28 April 2003 by Universal Music International Widescreen DVD: Universal 982575-0
Tracks: In The Flesh?; The Thin Ice; Another Brick In The Wall (Part 1); The Happiest Days Of Our Lives; Another Brick In The Wall (Part 2); Mother; Goodbye Blue Sky; Empty Spaces; Young Lust; One Of My Turns; Don't Leave Me Now; Another Brick In The Wall

(Part 3); Goodbye Cruel World; Hey You; Is There Anybody Out There?; Nobody Home; Vera; Bring The Boys Back Home; Comfortably Numb; In The Flesh; Run Like Hell; Waiting For The Worms; Stop; The Trial; The Tide Is Turning

On July 21, 1990, Waters kept his promise to perform *The Wall* in Berlin, if the real Berlin Wall ever came down.

The site of the concert was Potsdamer Platz, until recently a mined part of no-man's-land, but before then the heart of the old city. The concert was intended to raise funds for The Memorial Fund For Disaster Relief, a charity established by World War Two RAF veteran Leonard Cheshire to raise £5 for every life lost in the wars of this century, to fund emergency aid programmes. Waters was joined by an impressive list of celebrities, including Bryan Adams; The Band (Levon Helm, Rick Danko and Garth Hudson); Paul Carrack; Tim Curry; Thomas Dolby; Marianne Faithfull; Albert Finney; James Galway; Jerry Hall; The Hooters; Cyndi Lauper; Ute Lemper; Joni Mitchell; Paddy Moloney; Van Morrison; Sinead O'Connor; and The Scorpions, plus The Military Orchestra of the Soviet Army and The East Berlin Radio Orchestra and Choir, all orchestrated and conducted by Michael Kamen.

Although credited, 'Empty Spaces' was not performed, Waters instead opting to have Brian Adams sing 'What Shall We Do Now' at this point, just as it had been performed during the original *Wall* concerts. In order to end positively, Waters substituted 'The Tide Is Turning' for 'Outside The Wall'.

There were several problems during the live show, including a total loss of sound during 'Mother', but these were substituted in the broadcast and released versions with material recorded at the dress rehearsal and a post-midnight re-creation, after most of the audience had left.

The album spawned two singles, 'Another Brick In The Wall (Part Two)' (Mercury MER

332) and the very rare 'The Tide Is Turning' (MER 336). Both were edited versions, with album versions added to 12" and CD formats. 'Another Brick...' also boasted a live version of 'Run Like Hell' on the 7" and an atypical, studio-reworked 'Potsdamer Mix' of it on other formats. 'The Tide Is Turning' was backed by 'Nobody Home' from the same concert.

The film was at one time available as a '2 on 1' video with Pink Floyd's *The Wall* movie (Polygram Video 087 730 3). In May 2003, the album was released in hybrid CD/ Super Audio (SACD) format. A 4:3 format DVD was issued in 2003, with extras including a 30-minute documentary called *Behind The Wall* and the original animated films by Gerald Scarfe. A re-recorded 'Outside The Wall' was played over the closing credits. In May 2006 there was a new widescreen DVD edition, cropped from the earlier version, with 5.1 DTS surround-sound in addition to the earlier DVD version's Dolby 5.1 surround-sound and stereo tracks.

Although the concert was a massive spectacle, and all profits went to the charity, the resulting album – the only one from Waters' short relationship with Mercury – and

film are disappointing. The best advice is to go and buy a copy, in order to support the charity (or, better still, donate the full amount), then go home and play the original instead.

For a track-by-track analysis, see the entry for *The Wall*.

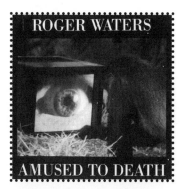

AMUSED TO DEATH

Released 7 September 1992
as Columbia COL 4 68761 2
Tracks: The Ballad Of Bill Hubbard; What God Wants, Part I; Perfect Sense, Part I; Perfect Sense, Part II; The Bravery Of Being Out Of Range; Late Home Tonight, Part I; Late Home Tonight, Part II; Too Much Rope; What God Wants, Part II; What God Wants, Part III; Watching TV; Three Wishes; It's A Miracle; Amused To Death

Waters worked, on and off, on this album for at least five years, originally announcing that it would be a continuation of the story-line of *Radio KAOS*. In early 1989, EMI announced that a planned release had been abandoned, stressing that this was only because Waters himself was unhappy with it, and promising a release "by early 1990". In the end, the album was released by Columbia – now a part of the Sony conglomerate, not an EMI subsidiary as it was when Pink Floyd recorded for them in the Sixties.

The plot was even more complicated than that of *Radio KAOS*, and would justify a book of considerable length all to itself, but no explanatory notes were provided, and the dearth of contemporary interviews has not helped. Basically, the story, which takes its title from Neil Postman's book *Amusing Ourselves To Death*, revolves around the "Soap Opera State" where more attention is paid to politicians' hair styles, suits, sex-lives and television manner than their policies. References were also made to the bombing of Libya by US planes based in England, the Tiananmen Square massacre, terrorist atrocities and the future discovery of the remains of the extinct Human species by alien anthropologists.

The album was dedicated to Private William Hubbard, whose colleague Alf Razzell was heard during the album's opening number, describing (on a television documentary) Hubbard's death in World War One. Waters again resorted to using lists for lyrics, but his worst sin was the stereotypical and sexist description of a Chinese dissident, his "yellow rose", as though her death only mattered because she was good looking.

Several numbers were graced by Jeff Beck, prompting Yardbirds fans to wonder when Waters, with a Clapton collaboration already under his belt, will record with Jimmy Page. Among the album's famous names were P.P. Arnold, John 'Rabbit' Bundrick, Rita Coolidge, N'Dea Davenport, Don Henley, Steve Lukather and Jeff Porcaro. A host of other musicians were also used, including old friends such as Michael Kamen, Andy Fairweather-Low, Graham Broad, Rick Di Fonzo, B.J. Cole, Katie Kissoon and Doreen Chanter, although Guy Pratt thought it politic to turn down an invitation to play bass! Surprisingly, Waters mostly restricts himself to vocals, playing only very little bass, acoustic guitar or synthesiser. The album uses QSound.

Waters was sufficiently bitter, when Bob Ezrin pulled out of the *Radio KAOS* sessions to work on *A Momentary Lapse...* instead, to include the lyric "Each man has his price, Bob/ and yours was pretty low". Patrick Leonard stepped into the void, co-producing with Waters, and also contributed keyboards. A multitude of studios were used, including The Billiard Room at Waters' London home, Compass Point in Nassau, Abbey Road, and eight others in London and the US.

After performing 'What God Wants' at The Guitar Legends festival in Seville and a charity concert in the US, Waters announced that he would tour with the album if it sold two million copies. Twelve months after its release, it had sold just over half that figure, and there was no tour.

Again, two singles were released. 'What God Wants, Part I (Video Edit)' (Columbia 658 139) came on 7", cassette and two CD formats, the second CD being in a box with colour prints taken from the promo video. There was no 12" release. The extra tracks were all from the album, as were all the tracks on the various formats of the second single, 'The Bravery Of Being Out Of Range' (658 819).

IN THE FLESH: LIVE

Released 5 December 2000
as Columbia COL 501137 2

Tracks: In The Flesh; The Happiest Days Of Our Lives; Another Brick In The Wall, Part II; Mother; Get Your Filthy Hands Off My Desert; Southampton Dock; Pigs On The Wing, Part 1; Dogs; Welcome To The Machine; Wish You Were Here; Shine On You Crazy Diamond, Pts. 1-8; Set The Controls For The Heart Of The Sun; Breathe (In The Air); Time; Money; Pros And Cons Of Hitch Hiking, Part 11 (AKA

5:06 AM Every Strangers Eyes); Perfect Sense (Parts 1 And 2); The Bravery Of Being Out Of Range; It's A Miracle; Amused To Death; Brain Damage; Eclipse; Comfortably Numb; Each Small Candle

Waters finally toured in July/August 1999, and again in June/July 2000, despite having no new album to promote. (The shows only took place in the USA and Canada; he would not reach the rest of the world until 2002.) He branded the tour *In The Flesh*, the same name used for Pink Floyd's 1977 tour to promote *Animals*. Several shows were recorded for this live album and DVD, with most of the material coming from the Rose Garden Arena, Portland, Oregon on June 27, 2000.

The band featured Waters' new guitarist and singer Doyle Bramhall II plus familiar cohorts Graham Broad, Jon Carin, Andy Fairweather-Low, Andy Wallace and Snowy White and singers Katie Kissoon, Susannah Melvoin and P. P. Arnold.

The album's opening track, which doesn't use a question mark, is actually a version of the opening track of the album version of *The Wall*, 'In The Flesh?', which has a question mark, and not the track on that album, called 'In The Flesh', without the question mark. No question.

'Each Small Candle' was one of two new songs performed on the tour (the other, 'Flickering Flame', does not appear here). The first stanza is variously attributed as the work of a South American torture victim or Danish poet Halfdan Rasmussen's work *Ikke Bødlen*. Neither is credited. The rest of the song tells the true story of a Serbian soldier who aided an injured Albanian woman.

The DVD also includes a backstage documentary, *Gearing Up*. In 2006, the CD and DVD were reissued in a combined package.

FLICKERING FLAME: THE SOLO YEARS VOL. 1

**Released 2 April 2002
as Columbia COL507906 2**
Tracks: Knockin' On Heaven's Door; Too Much Rope; The Tide Is Turning; Perfect Sense Part I & II; Three Wishes; 5.06 AM (Every Strangers Eyes); Who Needs Information; Each Small Candle; Flickering Flame (new demo); Towers Of Faith; Radio Waves; Lost Boys Calling (original demo)

This now-deleted compilation was one of a number of controversial discs, whose copy protection meant that they did not meet the CD specification and so could not be played on personal computers. There were also reports of problems playing them in some in-car and portable players.

All the tracks on the album segue from one to the next. The personnel, including those on the new recordings, were all uncredited.

'Knockin' On Heaven's Door', a cover of the Bob Dylan classic, was recorded for the soundtrack of the 1998 Israeli movie *Ha Dybbuk B'sde Hatapuchim Hakdoshim* (*The Dybbuk of Holy Apple Field*) and features Simon Chamberlain on keyboards, Clem Clempson (late of Humble Pie) on guitars and Katie Kissoon and Doreen Chanter's backing vocals, and was produced by Nick Griffiths.

'Flickering Flame' has Jon Carin on keyboards, Doyle Bramhall II on guitar and bass and was a joint Waters/ Griffiths production, and is the otherwise-unreleased song performed on Waters' 1999-2007 tours.

'Perfect Sense Part I & II' and 'Each Small Candle' are the live recordings from *In The Flesh: Live*.

'Lost Boys Calling' has music by Ennio Morricone and lyrics by Waters, with orchestration by Rick Wentworth. The finished version, produced by Patrick Leonard, appears on the soundtrack (Sony Classical SK 66767; released in 1999) to the 1998 Giuseppe Tornatore film *The Legend Of 1900* starring Tim Roth. The English and Italian (*La Leggenda del Pianista sull'Oceano;* soundtrack *Sony Music SK 60790*) versions of the film use different versions of the song, with different lyrics and harmonies, the former having additional guitar parts by Edward Van Halen. The DVD of the film includes the song's promo video, but note that while the US release has 5.1 sound on the movie, the UK's is only in stereo.

TO KILL THE CHILD / LEAVING BEIRUT

Released on 3 September 2004 as a download-only

In September 2004, Waters took the unusual step of releasing two new tracks as on-line downloads. Both have a strident anti-war message, and pleasant backing vocals by P.P. Arnold, Carol Kenyon, and Kate Kissoon. Andy Fairweather-Low supplies guitar and Graham Broad drums. Waters provides guitar, bass, keyboards and vocals, as well as yet more of his lists-as-lyrics.

The 3½ minute 'To Kill A Child' is a straightforward song. 'Leaving Beirut' is more unusual, featuring sung choruses between a spoken, prose narrative, complete with French dialogue. It describes, over 12½ minutes, Waters' true adventures while hitch-hiking in the Lebanon as a teenager, in 1961, and contrasting the hospitality he received with hostility our leaders now show to the people there. Waters' references to "wops" and "queers" sit uneasily with the song's intended message of tolerance and understanding, and it's otherwise undoubted worthiness does not stop it from being easier to read as a story, than to listen to. At least Waters seemed to think so, as performances on his 2006/7 dates dropped the spoken part, instead displaying the narrative as text, projected on to the screen behind the band.

A limited edition CD single was released in Japan, and people wanting to hear the tracks in proper CD quality, rather than heavily compressed, pay lots of money for copies. Its sleeve features a segment of Israel's despicable racial segregation wall, which Waters had visited and graffitied with the lyric from 'Another Brick… 2': "We don't need no thought control".

ÇA IRA

Released 27 September 2005
as: Sony Classical S2K 96439 (CD)
Sony Classical S2H 60867 (SACD)
Sony Classical S2K 93934
(CD, sung in French)

Act One
The Gathering Storm; Overture
Scene 1: A Garden In Vienna 1765; "Madame Antoine, Madame Antoine…"
Scene 2: Kings Sticks And Birds; "Honest Bird, Simple Bird…"; "I Want To Be King…"; "Let Us Break All The Shields…"
Scene 3: The Grievances Of The People
Scene 4: France In Disarray; "To Laugh Is To Know How To Live…"; "Slavers, Landlords, Bigots At Your Door…"
Scene 5: The Fall Of The Bastille; "To Freeze In The Dead Of Night…"; "So To The Streets In The Pouring Rain…"

Act Two
Scene 1: Dances And Marches; "Now Hear Ye!…"; "Flushed With Wine…"
Scene 2: The Letter; "My Dear Cousin Bourbon Of Spain…"; "The Ship Of State Is All At Sea…"
Scene 3: Silver Sugar And Indigo; "To The Windward Isles…"
Scene 4: The Papal Edict; "In Paris There's A Rumble Underground…"

Act Three
Scene 1: The Fugitive King; "But The Marquis Of Boulli Has A Trump Card Up His Sleeve…"; "To Take Your Hat Off…"; "The Echoes Never Fade From That Fusillade…"
Scene 2: Commune De Paris; "Vive La Commune De Paris…"; "The Assembly Is Confused…"
Scene 3: The Execution Of Louis Capet; "Adieu Louis For You It's Over…"
Scene 4: Marie Antoinette – The Last Night On Earth; "Adieu My Good And Tender Sister…"
Scene 5: Liberty; "And In The Bushes Where They Survive…"

Roger Waters' Opera, *Ça Ira,* has possibly the longest gestation period of any Pink Floyd-related project. In 1987, author and song-writer Étienne Roda-Gil (a friend of Roger Waters since 1968) and his wife, Nadine, approached Waters to see if he would set their opera libretto, which was in French, to music. Waters agreed, and a demo, made using string synthesisers, was completed and played to French President François Mitterrand in 1988. He wanted it to be performed at the French bicentennial the following July. This was resisted by the Opera Company's directors, and the opera was not premièred until 2005, when it was performed in Rome on November 17 (although the overture was performed by the Royal Philharmonic Concert Orchestra at a Countryside Alliance benefit concert at the Royal Albert Hall on October 16, 2002; and 15 minutes of pre-recorded highlights were played in Malta on May 1, 2004, the night it joined the European Union). By the time of the première, both Étienne and Nadine Roda-Gil were dead. There have since been a handful of other live productions, in Poland and the Ukraine.

In the process of recording the opera, Waters was persuaded by the record company to translate the libretto into English, and as such its surprisingly accessible, though it would be interesting to know how many Floyd fans have played it exactly once, or even not all the way through. The recording has very

Floyd-like use of spoken interjections, bird song, gunfire, and wind noises (created, like those on Floyd albums, using a VCS3 synthesiser). A couple of musical themes are borrowed from *Pros and Cons*.

The principal performers were Bryn Terfel, Huang Ying Paul Groves, Ismael Lo, Jamie Bower and Helen Russill. Orchestral and choral arrangements were by Waters and film composer Rick Wentworth, who also conducted the performers and co-produced the recording with Waters. Waters is not heard in the recording.

The recoding was released in three forms. The first was a three-disc set, the fist two discs containing regular CD and Super Audio (SACD) stereo and Dolby Digital 5.1 surround-sound versions of the opera, the third a bonus DVD with a 55-minute documentary by Adrian *"Live at Pompeii"* Maben, shadowing Waters over several years, as he worked on the opera, at first still in French, at his grand country house in Hampshire, and in the orchestral recording studio in Paris. This version also had a 60-page book with the libretto and credits, plus illustrations by Nadine Roda-Gil. The second version had just two regular audio CDs, containing the libretto and illustrations in CD-ROM form. Finally, there was a recording in the original French, also available in the regular CD format, on two discs.

THE LAST MIMZY ORIGINAL MOTION PICTURE SOUNDTRACK

Released 2 April 2007
as SilvaScreen SILCD1231
After meeting director Bob Sharpe at a party, Waters was invited to contribute a song, 'Hello (I Love You)' to the soundtrack of the feel-good sci-fi film *The Last Mimzy*. He co-wrote the music with Howard Shore, who also composed and conducted the film's score. The song opens with a child whispering "Is there anybody in there?" and includes the couplet "you can make your peace/ on the dark side of the Moon". For this one-off recording, Waters' band included Gerry Leonard (guitar) Steve Gadd (drums), Henry Hey (keyboard) and Rhiannon Leigh Wryn (the film's six-year-old star; additional vocals). Produced by Waters, Shore and James Guthrie, it closes the soundtrack album and was released as a mail-order only CD single (Silva Screen SILCD1236) on 26 March 2007, coupling the 'Radio Edit' and 'Album' versions. The promotional video for the song, including footage of Waters in the studio working on the – frankly disappointing – song, is an extra on the DVD of the film.

RICHARD WRIGHT

WET DREAM

Released September 22 1978
as Harvest SHVL 818
USA CD: Sony A24090
Tracks: Mediterranean C; Against The Odds;
Cat Cruise; Summer Elegy; Waves; Holiday;
Mad Yannis Dance; Drop In From The Top;
Pink's Song; Funky Deux

For his first solo album, Richard Wright took
Gilmour's advice and went to Superbear,
where he made this often overlooked, if
somewhat bland, record, accompanied by
top session musicians Mel Collins (sax)
Snowy White (guitar), Larry Steele (bass) and
Reg Isadore (drums). The sleeve was by
Hipgnosis. No singles were released from the
album, and Wright did not perform any
concerts.

The lyrics to 'Pink's Song' (not 'Against The
Odds', as stated on the US CD credits) were
written by Wright's then wife, Juliette, who as
Juliette Gale, was a singer with an early
incarnation of Pink Floyd, The Abdabs.
Appearances are not what they seem; the
song is actually about their children's tutor,
who happened to share his nickname with
the "star" of *The Wall*.

IDENTITY
(as Zee)

Released 9 April 1984
as Harvest SHSP 24 0101 1
(Not on CD)
Tracks: Confusion; Voices; Private Person;
Strange Rhythm; Cuts Like A Diamond;
By Touching; How Do You Do It; Seems We
Were Dreaming; Eyes Of A Gypsy' (on
cassette only)

After temporarily leaving Pink Floyd, Richard
Wright formed a short-lived partnership,
called Zee, with Dave Harris, former leader of
New Romantic band Fashion, with Wright
composing music for Harris' lyrics. The album
bears much more resemblance to the work
of Fashion than anything produced by Pink
Floyd. There were again no live dates. It was
never released in the USA and is the only
Floyd member's solo album never released
on CD anywhere.

'Confusion' was issued as a single, backed
by 'Eyes Of A Gypsy' (Harvest HAR 5227).
The 12" had an extended mix of the A-side
and a dub version of the B-side (12 HAR
5227).

BROKEN CHINA

**Released 7 October 1996
as EMI 8 53645 2**

Tracks: Breaking Water; Night Of A Thousand Furry Toys; Hidden Fear; Runaway; Unfair Ground; Satellite; Woman Of Custom; Interlude; Black Cloud; Far From The Harbour Wall; Drowning; Reaching For The Rail; Blue Room In Venice; Sweet July; Along The Shoreline; Breakthrough

Having regained his confidence with Pink Floyd, Richard Wright's surprise solo album was a tour de force, recounting his emotional response to supporting an unnamed "friend" (later revealed to be his wife) through clinical depression. Wright felt that two songs, expressing the point of view of the person with depression, needed to be sung by a woman who could empathise with the subject matter, and wisely chose Sinéad O'Connor, whose contributions to 'Reaching For The Rail' and 'Breakthrough' are perfect.

Floyd regular Tim Renwick was one of the album's three guitarists, seven tracks were co-written with Anthony Moore, who also wrote two of the songs, 'Runaway' and 'Woman Of Custom', by himself. 'Hidden Fear' and 'Blue Room in Venice' were written by Wright and Gerry Gordon, and the remaining seven tracks were by Wright alone. None of the lyrics were written by Wright. Other notable contributors included bassist Pino Palladino, drummer Manu Katché and Kate St. John, late of David Gilmour protégés The Dream Academy, on a variety of wind instruments. The album uses QSound and the cover was by Storm Thorgerson.

David Gilmour recorded an electric guitar part for 'Breakthrough', but it went unused, as Wright preferred Dominic Miller's acoustic alternative. There were clearly no hard feelings, as the song was performed at each of David Gilmour's 2002 shows, with Wright making a guest appearance to handle the vocals himself, as seen on the *David Gilmour In Concert* DVD.

There was one UK single, available as a 12" (EMI 12RW101) and as a promo-only CD (EMI CDRW101), released in October 1996, comprising three tracks: 'Runaway (R. Wright's Lemonade Mix)'; 'Runaway (Leggit dub)' and 'Night Of A Thousand Furry Animals (Inverted Gravy Mix)'. The first was a remox by the Orb (and still available on The Orb's *Auntie Aubrey's Excursions Beyond the Call of Duty Vol.2* (Deviant Records)); the other two were remixes by William Orbit with Matt Ducasse.

ANOTHER ALBUM?

At the time of his death, Wright was said to be working on a new album. Whether this work will ever see the light of day remains unknown.

BIOGRAPHY

Andy Mabbett was, for ten years, co-editor of *The Amazing Pudding*, the original, widely respected and now defunct Pink Floyd and Roger Waters magazine. He has written about them for several magazines, including *Q* and *Mojo,* co-authored *Pink Floyd – The Visual Documentary* and contributed to *Crazy Diamond – Syd Barrett and The Dawn Of Pink Floyd*. He also wrote the programme notes for Pink Floyd's induction in to the Rock and Roll Hall of Fame.